The Eroding Status-Quo
Power Struggles on the Temple Mount

Yitzhak Reiter

2017

The Eroding Status-Quo
Power Struggles on the Temple Mount

by
Yitzhak Reiter

Published by
JERUSALEM INSTITUTE FOR POLICY RESEARCH
and MULTIEDUCATOR, INC.
180 E. Prosepect Avenue • Mamaroneck, NY 10543

ISBN # 978-1-885881-50-2
© 2017 Yitzhak Reiter

Translation from Hebrew and Layout by Amy Erani

All Rights Reserved

The right of Yitzhak Reiter to be identified as author of this work has been asserted in accordance with the US 1976 Copyright 2007 Act and Israel's
חוק זכויות יוצרים, תשס"ח
No part of this book may be reproduced or utilized in any form or by any means, electronic or mechanical, or by any information storage and retrieval system without the prior permission of the publisher. The only exception to this prohibition is "fair use" as defined by U.S. copyright law.

"More than we are sovereigns over the Temple Mount, today we are its hostages."
(Prof. Shlomo Ben-Ami, Minister of the Public Security, 2000)

Jerusalem Institute for Policy Research,
Study no. 468

THE JERUSALEM INSTITUTE FOR POLICY RESEARCH–
BOARD OF DIRECTORS

Dan Halperin, Chairman of the Board
Ora Ahimeir
Avraham Asheri
David Brodet
Ruth Cheshin
Raanan Dinur
Prof. Hanoch Gutfreund
Dr. Ariel Halperin
Amb. Sallai Meridor
Gil Rivush
Dr. Ehud Shapira
Dr. Emanuel Sharon
Prof. Ilan Salomon

Director General: Lior Schillat

ACKNOWLEDGMENTS

This research, conducted in the Jerusalem Institute for Policy Research, was a by-product of a more comprehensive study on disputed holy sites funded by the Israel Science Foundation, Ashkelon Academic College, and the Truman Institute for the Advancement of Peace at the Hebrew University of Jerusalem.

My enormous thanks to the Jerusalem Institute for Policy Research and its former director, Meir Kraus, and the current director Lior Schillat, for the support and encouragement offered to me over the course of the years, and for the prevailing social and collegial atmosphere at the Institute. I also extend my thanks to Caroline Kahlenberg, who worked with me on the comprehensive research, of which one of the outcomes was this book.

My gratitude also extends to those institutes who have for years supported my research: Ashkelon Academic College and the Truman Institute.

Thanks to those who read and critiqued the Hebrew text, especially Dan Halperin and Meir Kraus, whose notes proved exceedingly helpful.

Finally, I am indebted to Amy Erani from MultiEducator Inc. who translated the book from its original Hebrew version and laid it out.

— Yitzhak Reiter

TABLE OF CONTENTS

Introduction 7

1. Sanctity of the Temple Mount/Al-Haram al-Sharif Prior to 1967 ... 13

2. Daily Life on the Temple Mount: Physical and Human Composition ... 17

3. "Status-Quo," as an Expression of Post-1967 Understandings 19

4. 'Live and Let Live': The Police and Waqf in Dialogue 25

5. Modus Vivendi, Tacit Understandings: 1967-1996 29

6. Collapse of the Modus Vivendi: 1996, 2000 55

7. Erosion of the Status-Quo and Creation of New Conditions Forged by Israeli Initiative, 2003-2015 95

8. October 2015 – Al-Aqsa Crisis and its Management 141

Summary and Conclusions 149

Endnotes 157

Bibliography 179

INTRODUCTION

In September 2015, on the eve of Rosh Hashanah, the Jewish New Year of 5776, tempers flared up once again at the Temple Mount/Al-Haram al-Sharif (TM/HS).[1] During the night, young Muslims had barricaded themselves inside Al-Aqsa Mosque and stockpiled stones, with the intent of disrupting visitation of Jews to the site. It was clear, in light of the upcoming holidays, that more Jews would be allowed to visit the Temple Mount than usual — a situation that the barricaded youth were determined to prevent. In their view, they were defending the pre-2000 status-quo at the holy compound and preventing its division between Muslims and Jews. They regarded the rising number of Jewish visitors accessing Al-Haram al-Sharif for ideological purposes, alongside the prohibition by the Israel Police against the entry of Muslims identified as "lawbreakers" and "defenders" (*murabitun* and *murabitat*), as an Israeli effort to Judaize the site.

Youth at the door to the eastern entrance of the Al-Aqsa Mosque (Author's collection)

Following orders of the Israeli government not to allow any disturbances or any disruptions of Jewish visitation, the police took effective action. Early in the morning the police stormed the TM/HS compound to blockade those who had fortified themselves in the mosque and arrest them. They also prevented Muslim worshippers from entering during visiting hours. A video clip showing Minister Uri Ariel in front of the Dome of the Rock, reciting the "Priestly Blessing" under police protection, was perceived by Muslims as a provocation and breach of the promises Prime Minister Benjamin Netanyahu made in November 2014 to King Abdullah of Jordan and U.S. Secretary of State John Kerry (i.e., not to permit visits by political figures and to prevent visitation of cabinet ministers and members of Knesset at the Temple Mount).[2] The photographs broadcasted from this holy site, showing policemen bursting into a smoke-filled Al-Aqsa, sparked harsh reactions in the Muslim world.[3] During the Jewish holiday of Sukkot, there was an outbreak of violence and terrorism in East Jerusalem and the West Bank. This wave of violence, which Palestinians termed the "Al-Quds Intifada," resulted in numerous deaths and injuries. As in the summer of 2014, this round of violence fueled tensions and tempers in 2015 as well. The U.S. Secretary of State arrived to mediate between the sides and reach agreements that mainly required compromise on Israel's part. It should be noted that many Palestinians claimed that the violence was primarily a response to events at Al-Aqsa.[4]

The person most concerned about this situation was King Abdullah II of Jordan. He issued a harsh warning stating "any more provocations in Jerusalem will affect the relationship between Jordan and Israel, and Jordan will unfortunately have no choice but to take action." King Abdullah added, "We have gotten reassurances from the Israeli government that this would not happen. However, regrettably, these are reassurances we have heard in the past."[5] The king spoke with U.S. Vice President Joe Biden and asked that the U.S. administration take measures opposing the continuation of Israeli policy at the Al-Aqsa Mosque, and bring an end to the Israel's aggressive behavior. The U.S. State Department issued a statement saying, "The United States is deeply concerned by the recent violence and escalating tensions surrounding the Haram Al-Sharif/Temple Mount."[6] Later on, King Abdullah said that the site belonged solely to Muslims alone, and it would be impossible for any prayer, other than Muslim, to take place there.

King Abdullah's custodianship over Islam's holy sites in Jerusalem received Palestinian and pan-Arab recognition on the basis of the agreement he signed with the chairman of the Palestinian Authority, Mahmoud Abbas, in April 2013. In its peace treaty with Jordan, Israel also recognized Jordan's special status vis-à-vis Islam's holy sites in Jerusalem.[7] Consequently, any action by Israel that is perceived as a violation of the status-quo undermined the legitimacy of King Abdullah and the Kingdom of Jordan. The internal political situation in Jordan, on the one hand, and proximity of the Islamic State's forces to the Hashemite Kingdom, on the other, endangers the stability of Jordan. Clashes at the Al-Aqsa Mosque also threaten the stability of the Hashemite Kingdom and its relations with Israel, because Abdullah II is seen in Arab eyes as responsible for protecting the site, yet, seems unable to dissuade Israel from acting as it does at the TM/HS. Given that Jordan and Israel have the same strategic interests,[8] disruption of the status-quo poses a threat to Jordan's stability, and thus could endanger Israel's long-term security interests along its eastern border. In other words, imposing full Israeli control over the TM/HS and opening the compound to ideological Jewish groups in increasingly larger numbers are violations of the accepted rules of conduct at the TM/HS. These practices come at a heavy cost for Israel: they would undermine its control over East Jerusalem and the West Bank, worsen Israel's relations with Jordan, and hurt Israel's standing in the international community. For example, as Prime Minister Netanyahu reported to the Knesset Foreign Relations and Defense Committee in October 2015, several cooperative endeavors with Sunni Arab states have been terminated because of tensions surrounding Al-Aqsa. Netanyahu added, "I'm uncomfortable about preventing my fellow ministers and Knesset members from visiting the Temple Mount, but the cost of violation might be that we are swept into a massive whirlpool, and that is unacceptable to me."[9] Israel's Prime Minister arrived at this conclusion only after the crisis had reached the point of a Palestinian uprising, in the form of a wave of stabbings, which required international intervention in order to calm the situation.

The events of September 2015 are only one link in the chain of events surrounding the TM/HS in recent years and eroded what had been the accepted status-quo. The conduct of each of the parties to the conflict reflects a lack of understanding regarding the essential meaning of status-quo at the TM/HS and of its inherent advantages. In addition, it undermines understandings reached earlier between Israel and Jordan regarding the TM/HS, to the point of posing a threat to strategic relations between the two states.

Furthermore, the understandings and status-quo arrangements regarding the TM/HS reached after June 1967 were never recorded in writing, according to former David District Commander of the Israeli Police, then Chief Superintendent Niso Shaham, who had previously headed the police unit responsible for holy sites. Shaham stated that Attorney General Elyakim Rubinstein considered putting the details of the status-quo in writing while he was Attorney General (1997 to 2004), but was persuaded not to do so.[10]

This study aims to lay the foundation for a well-thought-out Israeli policy regarding the TM/HS and to present alternative approaches to the authorities responsible for this sensitive site. The study analyzes changes that have taken place in the status-quo since 1967 and aims to provide policymakers with tools for managing the conflict and preventing violence at the site until a long-term solution to the dispute is found.

This study offers an overview of the current situation, which is viewed as the "status-quo" at the TM/HS, as well as the dynamics underpinning the changes that have taken place since June 1967. The understandings that have been reached will be analyzed, as will the accepted arrangements and subsequent disputes over day-to-day administration between Israel and the Muslim Waqf, which administers the compound.

A special effort is made in this study to understand the Arab/Muslim/Palestinian position regarding all aspects of the dynamics at this holy site in recent years. The study takes this approach because the Israeli leadership and public seem to be driven by national and identity-based motives with respect to the Temple Mount, without considering how these are perceived by the other side, and without taking into account the price Israel is paying and might continue to pay in the future as a consequence of erosion of the status-quo at the TM/HS.

CHAPTER 1
Sanctity of the Temple Mount and Arrangements of Access Prior to 1967

The Temple Mount is Judaism's principle holy site. It is identified with Mount Moriah in Jerusalem, where Abraham sacrificed his son Isaac. It has been sacred to Jews for roughly three thousand years, at the least since the days of the First and Second Temples [*Beit ha-Mikdash* in Hebrew], which stood for a combined total of about 850 years. From this arose the longing for Jerusalem throughout nearly two thousand years of exile, as articulated in prayers, ceremonies, beliefs, and the formation of Judaism itself.[11] The Temple Mount also holds great meaning to Christianity, for three reasons: According to the New Testament, Jesus visited the Temple, he preached that the place be purified, and there he envisioned its destruction. Since the early Church understood itself as an antithesis to Judaism, the site of Temple was not encompassed in the Roman and Byzantine city's boundaries. During the Crusader period, Christian worship returned to the Temple Mount. After the destruction of the Second Temple, the site was used as a literal dumping ground, remained outside the city area, and as far as we know Jews did not visit there.[12]

Early Islam identified the site of what Jews call the "Foundation Stone" with the Temple of Solomon. Toward the end of the seventh century, Caliph Abd al-Malik ibn Marwan built the memorial structure called the "Dome of the Rock" in recognition of how Islam was a continuation of Judaism and Christianity. The Muslim builders ascribed honor to a place that had been continuously held sacred for such a long time. For instance, the fifteenth century historian and Arab inhabitant of Jerusalem, Mujir al-Din, relates a story of an Islamic Preacher named Abu Bakr al-Vasiti and the book he wrote in praise of Jerusalem. Al-Vasiti wrote, "After David built many cities and the Children of Israel's circumstances improved, he wished to build *Bayt al-Maqdis,* and over the stone he would raise a dome in the place God sanctified in Aelia [Latin name for Jerusalem]." Elsewhere Mujir al-Din wrote, "Solomon built the *masjid Bayt al-Maqdis* according to his father David's command."[13] In his writings, Al-Vasiti quotes the tenth century Jerusalem historian Al-Muqaddasi, who recounts: "When Umar [Ibn al-Khattab, the second caliph] arrived at *Bayt al-Maqdis* mosque he said, 'I swear in Allah that this is the mosque of Sulayman son of Da'ud, peace be upon him. Our prophet wrote how he was transported to it [the Night Journey in the Quran, 17:1].'"[14] In 1951, historian and Palestinian official, Aref al-Aref wrote that Al-Haram al-Sharif was located on the same Mount Moriah recounted in the Book of Genesis. On that site stood the threshing-house of Araunah the Jebusite, which David purchased so he could build the Temple there, which Solomon built in 1007 BCE, and that structure was laying underneath the Al-Aqsa Mosque, remaining since Solomon's time. In 1961, Al-Aref added that the quarry outside of Damascus Gate was called "Solomon's Quarry," and that it was from there that David and Solomon supplied the stones for building the Temple.[15] Only in the twentieth century, with the outbreak of conflict between the Zionist and Arab/Palestinian movements, did the gradual tendency develop among Arab-Muslims to deny a Jewish connection to Jerusalem's Temple Mount.[16]

From the Jewish side as well, certain individual academics and some religious Zionists took to undervaluing the site's importance to Muslims. To this end, they pointed out how Jerusalem is not mentioned even once in the Quran, nor was it ever an Arab political capital.[17] Some Jews made these assertions despite the fact that Jerusalem was the direction to which the first Muslims prayed, and that it was there according to Muslim traditions where the prophet traveled on the back of the winged-steed Al-Buraq, and where, at the sacred stone, he ascended to heaven to meet the prophets that were his predecessors.[18] According to Muslim tradition, Caliph Umar ibn al-Khattab commanded that the rock be cleaned and that a mosque be built to its south, immediately after the city's capture in 636.[19] Caliph Muawiyah ibn Abu-Sufyan had his coronation there in 660 CE. It was Caliph Abd al-Malik ibn Marwan who built the dome, and his son Al-Walid who built a new Al-Aqsa Mosque from scratch, which had been a temporary structure until then.[20] Over the centuries, Muslim authorities built religious structures and various monuments in the area of Al-Haram al-Sharif and its nearby surroundings.[21]

There is some information indicating that Jews and Christians served in Al-Aqsa Mosque and the Temple Mount compound during the Middle Ages, and that some distinguished Jews visited the Mount on rare occasions—usually in exchange for bribes—however, these were the exceptions. Generally speaking, Jews were prohibited from ascending to the Temple Mount area during the period of Muslim rule over Jerusalem. During a portion of Mamluk rule (1250–1516) and under the

Ottomans (1516–1917) it was forbidden for Jews to even come close enough to look onto the Temple Mount.

During the first decade of British rule in Palestine, visitors of all faiths were permitted entrance to the TM/HS during established hours and with payment of an entrance fee. However, despite the arrangement that the Mandate government had organized, disputes broke out at the entrance to the TM/HS between Jews and Muslims, and these sometimes escalated into violence. Following the riots of 1929, the Supreme Muslim Council and the Islamic Waqf of Jerusalem prohibited Jews from entering the site's gates. The ban exacerbated tensions between the two communities on the access roads to the TM/HS, as well. Accounts from the 1930s tell us that the Supreme Muslim Council and Waqf administration permitted Jews and visitors from abroad to visit the TM/HS for a fee; thus economic considerations prevailed over nationalist and ethnic considerations. During the mandate period, Jewish leaders renewed ancient religious practices connected to the Temple Mount, though they were practiced at the Western Wall.[22] With the exception of VIPs, the ban on visitors continued until 1948 and persisted under Jordanian rule until June 1967.

CHAPTER 2
Daily Life on the Temple Mount: Physical and Human Composition

The Temple Mount is not just a holy site, a site of antiquity, or a symbolic focal point for the regional conflict. It is an area of 144 dunam (35.58 acres), containing dozens of structures and historical monuments, each with its own designated purpose. Any arrangement related to the rules of the compound should consider that the site is a vibrant place, where thousands of individuals arrive on a daily basis, and hundreds of thousands visit during Ramadan. The Waqf operates three schools inside the Haram: two for boys (elementary and high school) and one for girls.[23] Hundreds of educators are employed there, as well as two-hundred Waqf guards, Sharia judges, library workers, experts on preservation of ancient manuscripts, museum workers, an infirmary, firehouse, religious preachers and guides, Quran reciters, caretakers, janitorial staff, and preservation and maintenance staff, in addition to dozens of Israeli police officers.

The Al-Aqsa High School for Boys at the Northern Wall
The white doors are entrances to classrooms. (Photo: Elad Melamed)

The physical, organizational, and human characteristics of the TM/HS are impacted by the treatment of this sensitive site.

CHAPTER 3
"Status-quo" as an Expression of the Post–1967 Agreements

The "status-quo" regarding holy places is a legal concept pertaining to the holy sites, introduced in 1852 and 1856, by a decree (*firman*) of the Ottoman Sultan. The *firman* established the rights of Christian denominations at seven Christian holy sites in Jerusalem and Bethlehem, restoring the *status-quo ante* from a century prior (1757).[24] From that point on, the governmental position of 'freezing of the status-quo' gradually developed, as well as permanently fixing the religious practices of sites holy to more than one denomination, as a guarantee for the prevention of discord. However, there is a catch: the status-quo perpetuates the hegemony of entities whose political positions happened to be strong at a fleeting point in the past, and discriminates against those who held a weaker position at that moment in history. Jews, for instance, were banned from the Temple Mount for centuries, despite the fact of the site's primacy in Judaism.

Following the IDF victory in the Six Day War, there was no room to expect that the state of Israel would continue to discriminate against Jews and ban them from the Temple Mount. Alongside this were also the Israeli government's misgivings that granting Jews the right to pray on the Temple Mount, at that time, would lead to an increase in tensions, generating international pressure for Israeli withdrawal from East Jerusalem and the West Bank.[25] For this reason, the government did not permit non-Muslim visitors to pray at the site, allowing them to visit only as tourists. Israel even insured that Muslim prayers resumed in Al-Aqsa Mosque—within three weeks of its capture—and left the management of the Haram al-Sharif in the hands of the Jerusalem Islamic Waqf, to render it perfectly clear to the world it had no intentions of taking over this holy site. In addition, the government transformed the Western Wall, which in the Jewish national consciousness represents the Temple Mount, into the central site for Jewish religious practice. Consequently, the government demolished the residential area owned by the Mughrabi Waqf, and commissioned a wide plaza west of the Western Wall. The houses of the Abu-Sa'ud family, south of the plaza, were also demolished. Land owned by the Al-Khatuniyya Waqf was leased as well, allowing for archeological excavations that later became part of the Jerusalem Archeological Park.

What is called the "status-quo" for sites sacred to multiple faiths, therefore, is the prevailing situation at a particular time, determined by the opposing parties, who are careful not to institute any changes to the system or any of its component parts, such as: arrangements for access (including visiting hours, number of visits, areas of visitation, and rules of conduct), control over the area, hours of prayer, ritual, ceremonies religious or otherwise, rules of dress and conduct, administrative regulations and management, character of the site, and police and security protocols. Every change to any component of the status-quo is a potential incendiary spark for violence on the part of the wounded partner, a catalyst for a counter-reaction against the other side.

The new status-quo of 1967 began with a decision of the Israeli Ministerial Committee on Holy Sites. Appointed in August of 1967, it ordered the then-IDF Chief Rabbi, Major General Shlomo Goren, by way of the Defense Minister and Chief of Staff to "cease all actions connected to the organization of [Jewish] prayer, measurements, and the like on the Temple Mount." In this vein, the government also decided that, "When Jewish visitors enter through the gates of the Temple Mount for the sake of prayer, they shall be redirected by defense forces to the Western Wall." However, they did not institute an overall ban on Jewish prayer on the TM/HS.[26]

In 1967, the government of Israel began imposing Israeli law in East Jerusalem—including the TM/HS. Yet, Israel did not assume exclusive management of the site. Its sacredness to hundreds of millions of Muslims throughout the world, not to mention international policy considerations, brought Prime Minister Levi Eshkol to announce a continuation of the conduct, in which, according to him, the site's administration would belong to Muslim clergy, to the Islam Religious Endowments organization of Jordan, or the Waqf.[27] From June of 1967, a Jewish-Islamic *modus vivendi* developed, generally referred to as the 'status-quo', which included a series of mutually agreed upon understandings on the one hand, and a set of unresolved matters on the other hand. A continuous mechanism for communication and supervision took shape that oversaw the extent to which agreements were being kept, minimized confrontation, and dealt with crisis situations and emergency scenarios.[28]

A 'Modus Vivendi' is a temporary, unofficial arrangement designed to ensure a stable continuity of life. The modus vivendi of the TM/HS (also termed status quo) was an unofficial agreement, whose details were agreed upon in practice, in the field, through ongoing contact between the parties. The understanding was formed during periodic meetings between official Israeli authorities—mainly between the police and Jerusalem City Council (supervised by the Committee of Directors General, under the Committee of Ministers) and the members of the Muslim establishment who managed Al-Haram al-Sharif (the Waqf). At these meetings, all the details for how to administer the site were worked out, in effect, establishing a new set of norms, as it were, a new status-quo.[29]

The modus vivendi was reached thanks to two factors: First was the new balance of power, whose framework allowed each side to delineate its most crucial issues, while recognizing the 'red lines' of the other side. Second, the understanding between the two sides was agreed upon informally, orally, and at times, with tacit consent—in other words, sometimes one side pursues a course unilaterally, while the other simply refrains from responding. On the Israeli side, the the Chief Rabbinate supported the government's decision to redirect Jews wishing to pray on the Temple Mount towards the Western Wall. Their official halachic ruling and the sign they posted at the Mughrabi Gate, according to which entrance of Jews (to the Temple Mount) was prohibited by Jewish law, eased acceptance of the modus vivendi, which practically speaking, was a set of compromises and understandings.

Leaving administration of the TM/HS in Muslim hands softened international resistance to the steps Israel took, aided in normalizing Israeli control over the TM/HS and facilitated Israeli jurisdiction over East Jerusalem. Nevertheless, the annexation of East Jerusalem, as the start of Israeli rule, was never accepted internationally, certainly not by the Jordanians, Palestinians, and the rest of the Muslim world. These entities saw the circumstance of Israeli rule over East Jerusalem, as one of occupation according to international law, and 'Al-Aqsa's territory' as temporarily 'subjected to captivity.'

With regard to Muslim authorities, their perception of the 'temporary' nature of Al-Aqsa's 'captivity' allowed for Israel, the Palestinians and Jordanians to establish post-1967 understandings regarding management of the site. From Israel's perspective, the passive acceptance on the parts of the Jordanians and Palestinians, on arrangements which Israel imposed, made it possible for the Israeli government to claim its sovereignty was realized—except this sovereignty was revealed to be limited in scope.[30]

The post-1967 status-quo collapsed, in part, during September 1996, in the wake of the confrontation over the opening of the Northern exit to the Western Wall Tunnel. Ariel Sharon's protest-visit to the Temple Mount in September of 2000 caused the status-quo to collapse entirely. In the beginning of October of 2000, the TM/HS was closed to non-Muslim visitors for nearly three years. The area was reopened unilaterally by Israel in August 2003. However, entrance was still barred to the Al-Aqsa Mosque, the Dome of the Rock, the underground prayer halls, and the Islamic Museum. The weakening of the Palestinian Authority at that time allowed for Israeli authorities to enact more forceful policies, which provoked counter-reactions by

Muslims during the Second Intifada and afterwards. On the Jewish side, nationalistic-religious groups have exacerbated their actions since August 2003 (i.e., Temple Organizations encouraging group visits to the Temple Mount); while on the Muslim side, the activities of the Northern Branch of the Islamic Movement, Hizb al-Tahrir and the Hamas, together with the Jewish activities, forced a collapse of the previous set of agreements. This trajectory reached its apex during the events of October 2014 in East Jerusalem. Out of concern over increasing acts of violence throughout the city, the Israeli government (following a meeting in Jordan between King Abdullah II, Prime Minister Netanyahu, and US Secretary Kerry) chose to ban Israeli government ministers and members of Knesset from visiting the Temple Mount, and removed the age restrictions for Muslims accessing Al-Haram al-Sharif for Friday prayers. In spite of this, the status of TM/HS remained an explosive issue.

An analysis of the various developments that manifested around the TM/HS over the last two decades reveals how these developments are eroding the post-1967 arrangements, and impeding the status-quo, which had operated successfully during 1967–1996.

The analysis of the dynamics surrounding the TM/HS that follows relates to three different periods: The first was a period of continued mutual understanding and arrangements during 1967–1996; The second was the transitional period from 1996 to 2003, during which the modus vivendi of 1967 collapsed, to the extent that neither Jews nor any non-Muslims were allowed on the TM/HS; The final period was the erosion of the status-quo during the years 2003–2015.

CHAPTER 4
'Live and Let Live':
The Police and The Waqf in Dialogue

Officials in the Israeli establishment contend that Israel's strategy regarding the Temple Mount is designed from the bottom up. In other words: Problems are brought from the field to the political leadership, who discuss matters exclusively in times of crisis or with issues of pressing concern.[31] Once every three months, the Minister of Internal Security convenes meetings to provide an ongoing update of events taking place on the TM/HS. Apart from this, he has no dealings with the matter. It is the Israeli police officers, active in the field, who are in constant negotiation with the Waqf. The aim of the police is to keep things calm on the ground, and to that end they understand the necessity of maintaining good relations with the Waqf, and—at times—to acquiesce to reasonable requests, including those regarding matters of construction and maintenance.

The dialogue between police officers and directors of the Waqf is based on the principle of 'live and let live'. The State of Israel is represented on the ground by the police units at four levels: Commander of the Jerusalem District, Commander of the David Sub-district, Commander of the Holy Sites Unit, and Commander of the Temple Mount Unit — and Israel has the utmost interest in maintaining order and preventing violence. Likewise, both the Waqf and the Kingdom of Jordan are interested in keeping order, but they are also concerned with conducting their affairs efficiently, particularly in matters of conservation, maintenance, construction, and development. Both sides have the means to hurt one another. The police, for instance, could stop construction and maintenance, and the Waqf could let the reigns slip and permit violence to be perpetrated by Muslim youth.

Senior police officials related in closed conversations that police are forced to act and make decisions in highly sensitive situations without receiving directives from the government. As the ones on the front lines, the police are the entity that directs the ongoing contact with Waqf officials.

The level of confidence and mutual appreciation between the heads of the police and the Waqf at the TM/HS compound is impressive. In February 2016, the Waqf complained that thirty of its maintenance workers were not working, because the Israel Antiquities Authority would not allow them to initiate projects they had made requests to do long before. The backdrop to this was the government's (the Council of Ministers) avoidance of making decisions and its tendency to refuse work projects the Waqf requested to implement on the TM/HS—a situation which was liable to raise tensions and jeopardize relations between the sides. Thus, tensions continued until present day (2017).

The Temple Mount/Al-Haram al-Sharif is not a static site of antiquities, but a rather enormous, highly active, and multi-functioning venue, which demands continual maintenance and development. In one respect, the police enforce the law on the TM/HS, while on the other hand, they assist the Waqf in carrying out its maintenance, conservation, and development projects. The police and the Antiquities Authority make recommendations to the Ministerial Committee regarding construction and conservation projects. Some of their suggestions are driven by the need to preserve a beneficial dynamic, meant to reduce tension and to maintain stability and quiet at the site. The success of this dynamic is assured if representatives from both sides of the ongoing dialogue possess personalities conducive to friendly dialogue, trust, and good relations. It also depends on the ongoing activities of the police, the Antiquities Authority, the legal advisor to the government (also Attorney General), and the Ministerial Committee's ability to provide timely responses to ongoing matters. Additionally, the success of the dialogue is also dependent on the Waqf representative being a strong figure who knows the limits of negotiations and who receives the full support of Jordan.

CHAPTER 5
Modus Vivendi, Silent Agreements: 1967–1996

The period of tacit understandings is the most significant, given the simple fact that it persisted for thirty years, and was accepted by the various sides. It was this period that forged the binding of the 'status-quo,' at least according to Jordan and the PA. Israel's recognition of the responsibility of the Waqf to manage Al-Haram al-Sharif/Temple Mount, while maintaining the Israeli monopoly on security and policing, forced the sides to maintain dialogue and coordination. Over time, a routine of regular meetings took place between Waqf personnel and representatives of the Israeli police and Jerusalem Municipality, in which the two sides clandestinely discussed both ongoing concerns and matters raised on their own initiatives. It was in these meetings that tacit understandings were reached regarding current affairs, as well as specific episodes, which were communicated to and coordinated with governmental authorities in Israel and Jordan. Over time, these understandings turned into a modus vivendi, (which both sides refer to as the 'status-quo').

The particulars of the understandings from that time will be detailed below individually by topic: administration and upkeep; rules of conduct and dress; access, visitation and prayer; policing, security and preservation of public order; antiquities, conservation and construction; symbolic expressions and protests.

Administration and Maintenance

The continued administration of Muslim activities on the TM/HS rests in the hands of the Waqf,[32] which reports to Jordan. But, today, there are also employees who are openly identified with the PA, or, who are minimally required to maintain double loyalties. The Waqf maintains hundreds of employees at the site: unarmed guards, people who assist in religious services, who engage in repair projects, work in religious organizations, education, and tourism. The Waqf is responsible for Muslim activities including: ritual practice, various ceremonies and events, sermons, and study groups. They established the dress code and admission fees for the Dome of the Rock and Al-Aqsa mosque. We should recall that within Al-Haram al-Sharif there are buildings that have been used as places of housing for centuries, and in addition, that there are three active schools there. These operations complicate inspection and supervision at the entrances.

Rules of Conduct and Dress

The Jerusalem Islamic Waqf established rules such as obligating visitors to remove their shoes before entering the Dome of the Rock or Al-Aqsa mosque. Over time, with the increasing Islamization of the public sphere, they introduced stricter rules of dress for women, i.e., requiring a scarf to cover the head and shoulders and long dress or skirt, which the Waqf provides to visitors when they are allowed to enter the shrines.

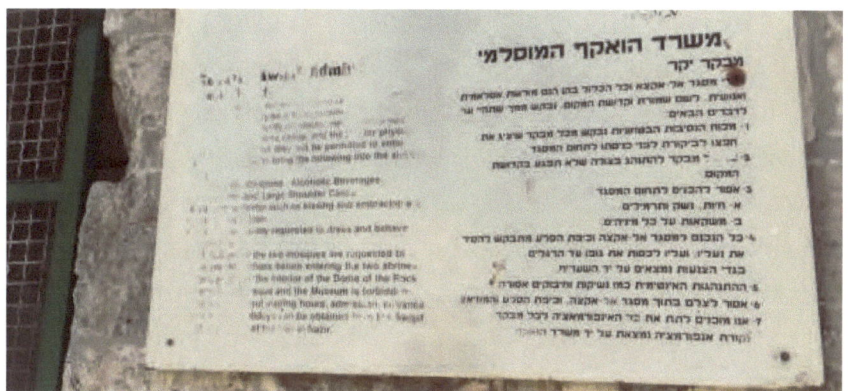

Sign indicating the Waqf rules of conduct by Mughrabi Gate (Photo by Author, 2 February 2016)

ACCESS, VISITATION, AND PRAYER

Muslim Access

Until 1996, Muslims could access Al-Haram al-Sharif without restrictions, as per the rules established by the Waqf. Israeli police assisted in enforcing the Waqf's rules at the entrance gates, though the police did curb freedom of access for non-local (West Bank and Gaza) Muslims, especially at sensitive times or based on intelligence warnings regarding the potential of violent outbreaks. In some cases, the police collected the identification cards of everyone entering for prayer—an act which was interpreted by Muslims as a method for reinforcing Israeli rule in the site, though the issue never reached a point of crisis.[33]

Jewish Access

One of the outstanding changes that the Israeli government enacted after 1967, was the legislation and only partial implementation of the law for the Protection of Holy Sites of 1967—which promises free access to holy sites, including the TM/HS.[34] At first, it allowed for the free access of non-Muslims to the TM/HS during times coordinated between the police and Waqf clerks: hours between Muslim prayers (7:30am-11:00am, 1:30pm-2:30pm on Sunday-to-Thursday, and one hour less during the winter).

What was called the 'status-quo arrangement' of 1967, allowing non-Muslims visitation, is a continuation of the same hours allotted for non-Muslim visitors, followed by the Jordanian police from 1950 to 1967. A Waqf guidebook from 1950 establishes possible visiting hours between 7:30am and 11:00am. These are the same primary visiting hours maintained after June 1967, with two distinctions: First, Israel did not allow the Waqf to collect admission to the esplanade, only to Al-Aqsa Mosque, the Dome of the Rock, and the Islamic Museum. Second, the arrangement between Israel and the Waqf established additional afternoon visitation hours, from 1:30-2:30 PM, following afternoon prayer.

It must be emphasized that in the status-quo arrangements of 1967, it was clear that Jews had the right to visit the site, but not to pray there. To this day, the Israeli police forbid Jewish prayer on the TM/HS. Thus, the post-1967 status-quo addresses Jewish visitors as tourists and not worshippers. The question then arises, whether Jewish groups or individuals seeking to change the status-quo out of their ideological motivations, meet the criterion to maintain their status as "visitors."

From 1993, the Israeli Supreme Court created a legal framework stating that while Jews had the right to pray on the Temple Mount, the police hold the authority to prevent the realization of that right. In the words of then-Chief Justice Aharon Barak, "The fundamental point from which we begin here, is that every Jew possesses the right to ascend the Temple Mount, pray there, and commune with his Creator. This is an inherent part of religious freedom. This is inherently part of freedom of speech."[35] Yet, in the same breath, the court ruled, "As with all human rights, this one is not fully absolute. It is a relative right. [...] In a place where the near-certainty exists that real damage will be inflicted on the public interest, if the human right to freedom of worship and expression are realized, we are permitted to restrict the human right, for the sake of safeguarding public order."[36] In 2006, it was even stated outright, by then Chief Justice Dorit Beinisch, "the authority of the police to block entrance to visitors and worshippers at the Temple Mount, under any case of definite and imminent danger, capable of inflicting severe damage to the public interests, derives from the police's explicit role of maintaining public order and security of life and property [...] authorizes police to forbid, or conditionally restrict, entrance to the TM/HS. Additionally, the police have authority, in given circumstances, to narrow the restrictions of entry or bar specific individuals, all for the sake of protecting public peace and security."[37]

On the basis of this ruling, it falls to the police to assess—on a daily basis—if such a danger is indeed present. Yet, they operated based on the assumption that danger on the TM/HS was constantly impending.

In June 1967, the TM/HS site's directors began collecting admission fees from non-Muslim tourists looking to enter the TM/HS. At first, Israelis were asked to pay half the admission price. In response, police expropriated the keys to the Mughrabi Gate from the Waqf and permitted Jews to enter that way without admission, since demanding an entrance fee stood in contradiction to Israeli law ensuring free access to holy sites. Waqf directors responded by shifting the ticket sales point inside the site, (technically speaking: visitors paid a fee for the 'Guidebook to Al-Haram al-Sharif'). Payment collected from non-Muslims entitled them to enter the Al-Aqsa Mosque, the Dome of the Rock, and the Islamic Museum, while visiting the open esplanade itself would remain free of charge.[38] In 2000, non-Muslims paid 25 NIS, or $6, for an entrance pass. This arrangement came to halt at the end of September that year.

In October 1990, Israeli police stormed the TM/HS in an action that ended with seventeen Muslims killed, due to a threat posed to the lives of two policemen who were surrounded by protesters and trapped in the police station in the compound. In response, the Waqf unilaterally chose to shut the gates earlier than had been done previously. Since the Israeli authorities never forced them to keep the site open the same hours as before, therefore, effectively, control of visitation times rested in the hands of the Waqf.

Jewish Prayer

Jews hold an ancient right to access and to prayer on the Temple Mount. The question to be asked is whether these rights were lost to them by force of historical circumstance, given that from the destruction of the Second Temple to the present day followed by the Islamic conquest of Jerusalem in AD 638—i.e., for the past 1,400 years (excluding the 88 years of Crusader rule)—the site has been used solely for Islamic worship. From the standpoint of Israel and most of the Jews in the world, Jews possess the right of access and right to worship on the Temple Mount, it being the holiest place for the Jewish people. However, the question of the realization of that right, in a manner that is neither peaceful nor agreed upon, in a place that has served as a Muslim prayer site for 1,400 years, becomes a question of political policy and security. So, Israel invented the distinction between 'the right of access' and the 'implementation of the right of worship,' and on the basis of this distinction it conducted dealings both with the local Waqf and the Kingdom of Jordan.

The Muslim world views Al-Haram al-Sharif as a place of Islamic prayer alone and fiercely resists Jewish worship there—among other things, for fear the issue might be exploited as a means for either obtaining Jewish control over the site, or dividing it. The ban issued by the majority of rabbinic authorities and the Chief Rabbinate, prohibiting Jews from entering the Temple Mount on grounds of "awe of the sacred," helped overcome the urge Jews had to take over the Temple Mount and to hold Jewish worship there after 1967.[39] The government did not permit Jews to pray there, nor did they arrange set hours for Jewish prayer services. They even blocked Jewish freedom of worship by handing the police and defense forces administrative orders, whose purpose was to protect the public peace and prevent bloodshed. The Israeli ambassador to the UN at that time said that Israel deliberately kept from establishing regular Jewish prayer on the Temple Mount so as not to offend the religious feelings of the Muslim populace, and to prevent strife between religious communities.[40]

Israeli courts also lent their support to government policy.[41] One ruling said, "Freedom of worship must be deferred in the face of the need to protect public order, even to the point of cancelling all ritual … Jewish religious worship at the Temple Mount."[42] With this, the Supreme Court found a need on numerous occasions to clarify that freedom of worship is a natural right implied within freedom of religion, and that freedom of access had no purpose if it did not include freedom of worship.[43] In 1976, Judge Ruth Or ruled on the matter of the Beitar youth movement who had prayed at the Temple Mount causing a riot. Her decision implied that Jews are entitled to pray on the TM/HS.[44] Muslims reacted to the ruling both in writing and in violent protest. Still, the Israeli police promised the Waqf that it would not permit Jewish prayer at the site. It should be noted that during the 1970s, discreet, individual Jewish prayer was allowed by the Waqf, who would turn a blind eye to it so long as it was done imperceptibly (though the Waqf deny this). But in 1980s, that custom stopped due to fears of violent outbreaks. On occasion, some radical Jewish activists have been successful at "sneaking in" prayer at the Temple Mount, which they have then filmed and uploaded to the Internet.

Israeli policy on the topic of Jewish prayer on the TM/HS is too vague. On the one hand, the Knesset passed a law that gives Jews a right to pray there, and on the other hand, the police prevent Jews from actualizing that right. This lack of clarity has contributed to the ongoing struggles of Jewish groups demanding to pray at the site.[45] The movements that champion Jewish ascent to the Temple Mount are not permitted to visit the TM/HS if police believe there is the slightest question of whether their presence would cause a severe disruption, and that their safety during their visit could not be guaranteed.[46] When members of these groups turned to the courts to demand their right to worship, the state responded that the non-actualization of the Jewish right to worship is part of the site's status-quo. Hence, for instance, when Superintendent Aryeh Brand, a senior plaintiff for the police, was asked how police would proceed if it were one hundred percent convinced that a solitary, silent prayer would end peacefully and without bloodshed, Brand responded that even if they were convinced in advance, the state would not allow it. When the judge asked why, Superintendent Brand replied, "Because we are bound to the status-quo."[47]

*The Mahkmah Building
(Madrasa Tankiziyya) (Photo by author, 2 February 2016)*

Attempts of radical Jewish elements to pray at the Temple Mount have not ceased from June 1967 to this day. In June 1967, Rabbi Shlomo Goren, Chief Rabbi of the IDF at that time, attempted to establish large-scale Jewish prayer on the Temple Mount, but it was denied to him by order of Defense Minister Moshe Dayan. In due course, after Rabbi Goren took off his uniform, he was permitted by several Ministers of Defense to pray communally on the second floor of the Mahkamah Building—a structure whose entrance lies outside the Temple Mount, a portion of which extends three meters into the area. The building was also controlled by the border police. Two of the upper rooms of the Makhamah were approved for use as a synagogue, and Rabbi Goren held the custom of praying there twice a year: on the Ninth of Av, the fast commemorating the destruction of the Temple, and on Yom Kippur.[48] His family and a group of a few dozen Jews continue that tradition.

Policing, Security, and Preservation of Public Order
TM/HS security is split between the Islamic Waqf Authorities—who employ upwards of two hundred guards who patrol the compound, working in three shifts 24/7—and the Israeli police, who maintain a permanent station inside the TM/HS, along with policemen stationed at the entrances and the Mahkamah Building which also serves as a post for observation and warning.[49] Until the mid-1980s, border-police frequently patrolled within the TM/HS, and members of the Waqf often complained about this and about inappropriate conduct on their part.[50] Following these complaints, the head of the Supreme Muslim Council, Sheikh Sa'd al-Din al-Alami, came to an agreement with the police commissioner at the time that the border police would be stationed only at the gates and would not enter into the area of the TM/HS except in cases of emergency.[51]

In the thirty years following the Six Day War, there were a number of violent incidents. The incidents were, however, anomalies, and the understandings the sides had reached allowed these incidents to be contained. The worst of these events were the following: In August 1968, Michael Denis Rohan, an Australian tourist and messianist, set fire to a portion of Al-Aqsa Mosque; In 1981, a Jewish underground cell was uncovered that had plotted to bomb the Dome of the Rock; In 1982, a uniformed soldier opened fire into Al-Haram al-Sharif; The violent protests of the First Intifada over TM/HS, and in October of 1990, police were forced to break into the Temple Mount to rescue two policemen surrounded by a furious mob – an incident ending with the deaths of seventeen Muslims and many more wounded.

One of the lessons of October 1990 led to the founding of a special police unit for the Temple Mount, comprising 80 officers—24 of them posted at the entrance to the Mount during the day, and another 17 at night.[52] The Waqf rejected police requests to install cameras and electronic security devices at various locations on TM/HS site. They were concerned that if the issue were made known, it would be perceived as recognition of Israeli sovereignty. However, in 2013 the situation changed, as will be explained in chapter 7.

Preservation of Antiquities and Construction

The particular sensitivity of the TM/HS, that it is sacred to more than one religion, necessitates careful use of judgment and extreme caution with everything regarding its physical condition, the character and methods of conservation, preservation, excavation, construction, demolition or any other change made there. There are two sides to this issue: the physical site itself, and the rules of conduct to be followed when you perform any kind of action.

From the Israeli perspective, the Antiquities Law and the Planning & Building Law apply equally to the TM/HS. Anyone looking to begin work is required to seek approval from the Antiquities Authority and the Committee of Planning and Building. But the Waqf does not recognize this authority, as it does not recognize the application of Israeli law, since in their view the site falls under the definition of occupied territory, which constitutes a breach of international law. Therefore, the Muslims consider themselves free to initiate any development projects or physical alterations on the Haram al-Sharif, disregarding Israeli law. They claim the Waqf has its own archeologist, and that they are not subject to the Antiquities Law. They rely on the laws of the British Mandate Order-in-Council. In any event, if they are subject to law, in their opinion, that would be Jordanian law, which does not forbid work on Al-Haram al-Sharif.[53] Together with all this, there is also a long-standing agreement that the Waqf gives advance notice to the Israeli police of their intentions to initiate projects. This notification is a general one, separate from the legal process and containing no plans for the work to be initiated. According to Police Commander Avi Bitton, who was in charge of the David sub-district, the Waqf, for its own reasons, is not prepared to submit a request to the Planning Committee, suspecting that if the matter became public knowledge, it would be seen as recognition of Israeli sovereignty over Al-Haram al-Sharif. For this reason, the Israeli police submit the Waqf's applications for construction, conservation, or renovation to the authorities, and the Antiquities Authority signs off on the requests.[54]

Until the 1990s, the Waqf protected the site's character and allowed representatives of the Israel Antiquities Authority to visit and inspect the site. From 1986 onward, the movement of 'Temple Mount Faithful' began complaining of legal violations perpetrated by the Waqf at the TM/HS.⁵⁵ Yet the projects initiated by the Waqf, up until then, were minor ones compared to those it initiated in the latter half of the 1990s: they renovated buildings, installed prayer platforms, and erected a monument in memory of those killed in the 1982 Sabra and Shatilla massacre of Palestinians in Lebanon.

Unoccupied prayer platform (mastaba) commemorating the dead of the Sabra and Shatilla refugee camps in Lebanon (Author's collection)

The Waqf views the areas surrounding the TM/HS as part of Al-Haram al-Sharif itself, which is why conflicts erupt each time Israel implements archeological digs or tourism projects to the south and west of the TM/HS site. From the perspective of the Palestinians, the archeological digs or tourist enterprises that Israel conducts there are intended to strengthen the Jewish historical narrative, as a basis for claiming ownership of the site.

In 1969, Israel began excavation of the Western Wall Tunnel, which runs from the Western Wall Plaza northward alongside the border wall of the TM/HS. The excavation was conducted under the initiative of the Ministry of Religion, without archeological supervision, and not as part of organized archaeological research. The tunnel was perceived by the Waqf as a threat to Muslim rights on Al-Haram al-Sharif. The changes brought about by Israel provoked indignation, and was one reason for the UNESCO declaration of the Old City of Jerusalem and its walls as a 'World Heritage Site in Danger.'[56]

In the early 1970s, Israeli officials purchased leasing rights for an area in the southern portion of TM/HS from the directors of Al-Khatuniyya Waqf and conducted archeological excavations and made physical changes intended to improve the tourism infrastructure of the site. The dig uncovered remnants of various periods in Jerusalem's history, including: vestiges of the Byzantine and Eastern Roman empires, buildings and palaces from the Umayyads and burial sites from the Abbasid period. Additionally, they revealed fragments and structures dated back to the Second Temple—the early Roman period. The area of the archeological excavation was approved to become a park, and was named "The Jerusalem Archeological Park."[57]

The Waqf vehemently opposed the excavations, out of fear that unearthing objects from early Jewish periods would alter the character of the surrounding areas of the site. Their opposition also stemmed from the fact that reinforcing the Jewish narrative could lead to the demand for occupation of and assumption of control over the TM/HS, and would strengthen the Jewish elements demanding a change in the status-quo. The Waqf also worried that underground excavation might damage the foundations of Muslim structures. Mainly, the Waqf was anxious that the Jews might open an underground passageway onto the TM/HS, or establish a Jewish prayer site on the lower levels.[58] To ease their anxiety over the ramifications of the Western Wall Tunnel, the Israeli authorities in charge invited directors of the Waqf on a covert tour of the tunnel. The tour eased tensions on the matter, for a time; however, judging by the actions of the Muslims in the 1990s, it would seem their fears even increased.

The rescue excavations done around the Mughrabi Gate in 2007 (for construction of the new bridge) is one more example of what concerned Muslims. It is not unlikely that the stated concerns— i.e., that the work would harm artifacts from the Muslim period— were merely a cover for their real fear that the construction might unearth new finds from the Second Temple period. For instance, there was the possibility of uncovering Barclay's Gate, a sealed entrance to the Temple Mount used in the time of Herod.

Mughrabi gate, viewed from the Temple Mount to its left. To its right is the staircase to Barclay Gate and the place of Al Buraq's ascent (Photo by the author)

The scientific excavations at the southern sector of the TM/HS contributed to the discoveries made from multiple historical periods, including the early Muslim period. Moreover, there was no basis to the fears of Muslim leaders that these excavations were a front for attempts to penetrate the TM/HS from below. In contrast, there was nominal basis to their concerns regarding the Western Wall Tunnel, which was dug under the initiative of the Ministry of Religions, and whose aims were not scientific, but contained a mixture of political and economic considerations—further mingled with simple curiosity and a wish to expand the territory. Thus, in August 1981, for example, the Rabbi of the Western Wall, who was responsible for the tunnel's excavation, announced the burrowing of a separate passageway running east from the northern section. Muslims saw the Jewish tunneling as an attempt to capture Al-Haram al-Sharif and to destroy the compound. They put out a call for mass numbers of people to come to Al-Haram al-Sharif to demonstrate their control over the mosque and protect it.[59] The episode raised fears that severe riots might result, so the men of the Waqf entered the tunnel under the protection of the police, sealed it with concrete, and flooded it with water.[60] The incident resembles that of the "Little Western Wall": In January 1986, the Ateret Cohanim organization uncovered the continuation of the Western Wall, near the Iron Gate Street. Members of the organization used to pray at what became called 'the Little Western Wall.' The men of the Waqf discovered a fissure extending from one of the entrances there, toward the direction of the TM/HS. The lack of understanding between these two factions almost resulted in bloodshed.[61] The professional opinion of the Jerusalem civil engineer revealed some basis to the claims that the foundations for ancient Muslim structures nearby were undermined. The complaints of the Waqf were heard and attended to, and the damage was repaired by the municipality.[62]

Another point of friction was the changes made to the Mughrabi Gate – the western entrance to the TM/HS, to which the police hold the keys. In 1978, Israel representatives painted the gate. The Supreme Muslim Authority protested, referring to the paint-job as "an act of aggression towards Al-Haram, and an attempt to alter its Muslim character."[63] In the 2000s, the 'Mughrabi ramp,' and the bridge that came to replace it, became the basis for controversy, which will be expanded upon in Chapter 7.

In July 1988 the Israeli government first announced its intention to open an exit for the Western Wall Tunnel by one of the northern gates of the TM/HS. The heads of the Waqf responded with a call to the masses to come and defend Al-Haram al-Sharif, and violent clashes erupted very quickly between Jews and Arabs in the Old City. As a result, the government was forced to suspend its plans.[64] It seems that the conflicts of July 1988 did not set off a warning light for government leaders, as evidenced by the events of September 1996, which will be described in this chapter.

Protests and symbolic expressions

One of the covert understandings that materialized after 1967 was the ban on displaying flags, national or otherwise, within the confines of the TM/HS.[65] Minister of Defense Moshe Dayan ordered the removal of the Israeli flag that had been raised over the Dome of the Rock immediately after its capture.[66] Palestinian sources claim Dayan did so in the wake of the strong protests from the Turkish consul in Jerusalem.[67] At the same time, the TM/HS became a center for political demonstrations, during which flags would often be raised or burned in protest. Organized Jewish groups, like the Temple Mount Faithful and the *Hai VeKayam* movement held occasional rallies, marches, prayer sessions, and raised flags, near the gates of the site, on the outer side, and attempted to ascend and to perform demonstrative religious rituals on the Temple Mount.[68] Yet the main demonstrations of protest at the site are held under Palestinian initiative. The Friday sermons at the Al-Aqsa Mosque, broadcast over a sound system throughout the entire compound, included provocative political messages. Attempts of the administration of the Israeli Military immediately after 1967, followed by attempts of the Ministry of Religious Affairs, to demand preachers in the mosques provide advance copies of the text of their sermons in order to censor sections aimed to incite, encountered vehement opposition from preachers and from the Muslim religious establishment. This domain lies fully in the hands of the Muslim Waqf employees.

Demonstrations that included the waving of PLO flags have often occurred on the TM/HS on many occasions. Some were arranged as protests of general national issues, while others were in response to specific Israeli actions taken on Al-Haram al-Sharif.[69] In February 1987, for example, there were solidarity rallies with the Palestinians in Lebanon—protests that progressed into violent clashes, in which police were wounded.[70] In the first year of the First Intifada, most of these demonstrations took place following Friday prayers, where anti-Israel slogans were chanted, PLO flags waved, Israeli and American flags burned, and stones thrown at both the security forces and Jewish worshippers at the Western Wall. The police and border-policemen were forced to enter and disperse demonstrations at the TM/HS on multiple occasions.[71] Another example, on November 15, 1988 when Yasser Arafat declared in Algiers the founding of a Palestinian State in front of the 19th Palestinian National Council, the heads of the Waqf convened a solidarity conference at the gates of the Al-Aqsa mosque and signed their own declaration of independence.[72]

The door to the left is the entrance to the Abu-Sa`ud house adjacent to the Mughrabi Gate, the house in which Arafat claimed to have been raised (Photo by Author, 2 February 2016)

One of the most turbulent demonstrations to take place on TM/HS happened on October 8, 1990, in the year that marked twenty-three years of Israeli rule over East Jerusalem. The Gulf crisis (the Iraqi invasion of Kuwait) had just begun, which injected fresh blood into the veins of the Intifada that had started in December 1987 and was active in the West Bank, Gaza, and Jerusalem. The situation in the Gulf awakened nationalist sentiments among Palestinians, as well as aroused a flurry of remarks from Jewish rabbis and religious figures who saw developments in the Gulf as signs of coming of the Messiah. It was in August 1990, against the backdrop of these incidents that police sent out an alert warning that these events might cause extremist elements to take action on the TM/HS. At that same time, two events of paramount importance took place in the Jewish-Arab sector. Fatah and Hamas, two of the central Palestinian organizations, who had been opponents of one another, successfully reached a mutual agreement for reconciliation and cooperation. The actions of Muslim youths on Al-Haram al-Sharif, which until then had been characterized along nationalistic lines, would from then on have a religious character.

The second incident was the announcement that the 'Temple Mount Faithful' movement was planning to lay a cornerstone for the Third Temple, near Dung Gate, and set up a Sukkah, a traditional booth for the holiday of *Sukkot*, by the Mughrabi Gate.

The announcement provided Hamas and Fatah with a good pretext for their first joint action on the sacred compound. On Friday, October 5th, there was already a visible escalation on the ground. Hamas distributed leaflets, and after prayers at the Al-Aqsa Mosque, the call of the *muezzin* went out to thousands of the faithful to come to the Mount in three days to prevent the Jews (of the 'Temple Mount Faithful' under the leadership of Gershon Salomon), from laying their cornerstone for their temple at Al-Haram al-Sharif.

The police did not permit Salomon's group to implement their plans. However, the police did allow them to hold the water-drawing ceremony at the Siloam tunnel. The contemporary celebration commemorates a ceremony performed during the Temple era, when water would be drawn from the aqueduct in a bronze urn. The *Kohen HaGadol*, High Priest, sprinkled water on himself, and the gathered faithful responded with song and dance. It should be recalled that a year earlier, Salomon's group held a similar event that provoked severe riots.

Despite the police's conciliatory announcements that they had no intention of allowing the Temple Mount Faithful near the Temple Mount gates, the Waqf leadership called on the masses to come—before it was too late, i.e., during the Jewish holidays—and use their bodies to block the Jewish attempt to wrest control of the site. The police devoted their attention to keeping Salomon's group secure and safe, and not necessarily to what was happening on the TM/HS. The police were unprepared for events on the scale that developed. On the morning of October 8, there were already roughly 10,000 Jewish worshippers in the Western Wall Plaza, gathered in preparation for hearing the Priestly Blessing. On the TM/HS itself were a handful of Muslim believers, situated in the plaza in front of Al-Aqsa Mosque, and they began gathering and piling up stones. After a few hours they began lobbying and throwing stones at police. Schools in the region announced a cancellation of studies for the day, urging their students to go to the holy place, where the preachers inflamed the Muslim worshippers. At roughly ten in the morning, about 30,000 Jewish worshippers were gathered in the Western Wall Plaza. Officers of the border police and other policemen tried to alleviate the extreme tensions there through talks with the Waqf leadership. The police had the impression that the men of the Waqf and the Arab leadership understood that Salomon's group would not enter the TM/HS. Yet in retrospect, it seems that the message was not transmitted to those gathered in the holy esplanade, who continued to exhibit increased signs of hostility.

At that same time, the Priestly Blessing was being recited, and as thousands of Jews left the Western Wall Plaza, the fuse was lit that ignited the fire in the area near the Dome of the Rock. A border guard stationed above the Western Wall, facing Al-Haram al-Sharif, accidentally let a gas grenade slip from his hands, which rolled towards a group of Muslim women. The Muslim masses who were listening at that time to religious and nationalist preaching over the loudspeakers stormed the border policemen. In five minutes, the crowds pushed the police out towards the Western Wall and through the Mughrabi Gate, throwing anything coming to hand at the police, and into the Western Wall Plaza behind them. The police responded, but tear gas and rubber bullets were ineffective, and the order was given to withdraw. The force retreated; however, two policemen were trapped in the police station at the northern end of the Mount. After numerous attempts to extract them, the commander managed to break through, and was followed by a police assault team. Facing them stood hundreds of Muslims armed with stones and clubs, who did not hesitate to attack police at close range, endangering both their own lives and the lives of the police. Many on the police force, who were shocked by the magnitude of the resistance, readied their weapons and opened fire toward the crowd, shooting bursts of live ammunition, rubber bullets and tear gas. At the first volley, dozens of the attackers fell, stunned by the intensity of the Israeli response.

Many of the police fired live rounds at rioters. Some were hit in the legs, some in their torsos. In a less charged scenario, the police would have chosen a more moderate means of dispersing the rioters, but this time their actions were determined by the threat to lives of their trapped friends. In every sense of the word, the TM/HS became a battlefield. At 11:25 AM, when the order was given to cease fire, the grim results were revealed: 17 dead Palestinians, over 100 wounded, 53 transported to hospitals—and an additional 34 Jewish worshippers and policemen were wounded after being struck by stones or various other objects, 28 of whom required hospital treatment. It was the most violent and deadly clash the Temple Mount had known since it was captured by Israel in June 1967.[73]

The events of October 1990, referred to by the Muslims as the "Al-Aqsa Massacre," were, at that time, a significant propaganda tool for spreading the slogan "Al-Aqsa is in Danger." Following the incident, numerous organizations and states—including the European Parliament and American government—released strong condemnations against Israel over its actions at an Islamic holy site. The UN Security Council unanimously accepted a resolution condemning acts of violence by Israeli forces that caused loss of life and injury to numerous Muslims on the TM/HS. The Security Council decided to send a fact-finding mission to Jerusalem, on behalf of the UN Secretary-General, and with the support of the United States. However, Israel refused to receive the delegation.

"The Al-Aqsa Massacre and the Great Challenge":
Title of a book published in Acre, following the events of October 1990

In summary, since June 1967, a tacit understanding took shape between Israeli authorities and the Waqf administration, which reported to the Jordanian government. By these agreements, Israelis were permitted to enter the TM/HS as tourists—generally through the Mughrabi Gate and during established visiting hours—but not to pray there. Likewise, the procedures were set pertaining to security at the gates of the TM/HS, the outer perimeter, and in cases of emergency, inside the compound. For its part, the Waqf saw these arrangements as the expression of a state of temporary occupation, and did not officially recognize the applicability of Israeli law on Al-Haram al-Sharif. However, the Waqf did properly coordinate the implementation of informal inspection of physical work in the area and antiquity conservation with the Israeli police. This series of agreements generally prevented outbreaks of violence and also made it possible to calm tense situations that developed after crises took place in and around the sacred shrine. The modus vivendi required the Israeli government to consciously relinquish full sovereignty over the TM/HS and the right for Jews to worship at the site. The Temple Mount is administrated by the Waqf, who established the rules of conduct and dress, hours of operation, sermon content, and other indications of governance and directorship. Israel, for its part, preferred tacit agreements that ensured public order, while concealing the fact that the State of Israel's laws were not formally enforced on the Temple Mount. These circumstances remained in place for 30 years, until the northern exit to the Western Wall Tunnel was opened, as is described in the next chapter. The depiction of the modus vivendi portrayed above will serve as a touchstone for understanding the changes that occurred after 1996.

CHAPTER 6
Collapse of the Modus-Vivendi: 1996 – 2003

The Oslo Accords had an indirect effect on the situation at the TM/HS. The Palestinian Authority, established in 1994, opted to become part of the administration of Al-Haram al-Sharif and acted to limit the position of Jordan at the site. However, a dramatic change in the status-quo took place in September 1996, when the tacit understandings between Israel and the Waqf collapsed and coordination between the two weakened. The collapse of understandings occurred around what the parties interpreted as egregious violations of the status-quo in the domain of public works. Therefore, this chapter begins with a description of this issue.

Construction Work and Maintenance of Antiquities
Following the opening of an exit to the Western Wall tunnel, the fears of the Islamic Waqf strengthened that Israel sought to turn Solomon's Stables into a Jewish prayer site by opening the Huldah Gates.[74]

In the middle of the 1990s, the Northern Islamic Movement, in cooperation with the Waqf, built an underground prayer hall in Solomon's Stables without requesting approval from the Israeli authorities. The construction was started by the Waqf Administration in 1996, in cooperation with the Northern Division of the Islamic Movement in Israel led by Sheikh Raed Salah, who served then as the mayor of Umm al-Fahm. The work was meant to prepare Solomon's Stables to function as an underground prayer hall and accommodate a large number of worshipers. From the perspective of the Islamic establishment, bringing a large number of worshipers to Al-Haram al-Sharif on Fridays reinforced and strengthened the Muslim character of the site and allowed Muslims to respond forcefully to any matter they perceived as causing damage or constituting desecration perpetrated by Jews.[75] Likewise, the large number of worshipers increased the holy status of the site and imbued the Waqf and Islamic Movement with political power. As such, it was important for Muslims to maximize the prayer areas in Al-Haram al-Sharif, especially the indoor spaces.

An additional reason for preparation of the underground prayer space was the suspicion that Jewish groups intended to invade or demand space for Jewish prayer on the lower level of the Temple Mount, or elsewhere, within the framework of final-status agreement with the Palestinians, and that the archaeological excavations, as well as the digging of the tunnels by Israeli authorities, were intended to invade the underground area of Al-Haram al-Sharif and undermine the foundations of the mosques.[76]

During the month of Ramadan, January 1996, Waqf representative attempted to explain the opening of the hall in Solomon's Stables for prayer (initially, in the absence of extensive renovations), based on an informal understanding with government representatives, similar to other understandings reached between representatives of the parties. The Minister of Internal Security at the time, Moshe Shahal, instructed his representatives, on the advice of Prime Minister Shimon Peres, to meet with representatives of the Muslim establishment on the TM/HS to approve their request, and at the same to inform them of the intention to breach the Western Wall's tunnel exit. The breakthrough of an opening at the northern end was designed to allow many tourists to explore its length, entering next to the Western Wall and exiting from the northern entrance amidst the Old City. The perception of Israeli authorities was that the tunnel was not a holy place and was not connected to the Temple Mount, so there was no need to request consent from the Waqf representative, and therefore, the matter was raised solely as a notification. In terms of the Waqf, the Western Wall, the tunnel, and the over-all area surrounding Al-Haram al-Sharif are an integral part of their holy site. Every change in the surroundings from what it currently is constitutes an attack on the status-quo, and more specifically, on the accepted modus vivendi.

The two issues, the construction of Solomon's Stables and the opening of an outlet from the Western Wall tunnel were raised together at one meeting, aimed at achieving a tacit understanding, or a trade-off deal, similar to the other understandings reached between the Waqf authorities and Israel at that time. However, in the case of the tunnel, Muslim consent was not requested, as it was obvious to the Israeli authorities that permission would not be granted—and they only expected that by giving this notification the tunnel's opening would not be followed by mass-scale riots. According to police, none of the Waqf representatives who attended the meeting responded to the announcement that the tunnel would be opened either positively or negatively.[77]

The attempt to gain an understanding about the opening of the Western Wall tunnel failed because the Jerusalem District Police Commander tried to deviate from the methods of previous agreements, based on which all the understandings were reached informally and verbally.[78] On January 24, 1996, the police commander sent a letter to Sheikh Abd al-Azim Salhab, Chair of the Council of Endowments,[79] and to Adnan al-Husseini, director of the Waqf in the Jerusalem District—both of whom were appointed by Jordan, but continued to serve, despite the Palestinian Authority's involvement (Hassan Tahboub, Palestinian Authority Minister of Waqf Affairs was present at the meeting, but was not a recipient of the letter.) In the letter, the police commander said, among other things:

> In the course of the meeting you requested to open Solomon's Stables, due to expected heavy rains and the concern for Friday worshipers during this year's blessed Ramadan. In response to your request, I have agreed to the opening of the space to the worshiping public, during the blessed month of Ramadan this year, in accordance with your commitment to limit the number of worshipers descending to that space, along with your acceptance of responsibility for what happens in the space, given the difficult conditions, which might endanger the safety of the worshipers, despite the appointment of ushers who will limit the number of worshipers at the site. During the meeting I stated that the atmosphere of peace prevailing in the region paves the way for the opening of the Western Wall tunnel to achieve economic goals and increase

tourist traffic, which will serve the general interest and which I will implement soon.

This letter invited a written response from Sheikh Abd al-Azim Salhad on February 3, 1996, in which he wrote among other things:

> This place [Solomon's Stables], like the mosque [the gates of the TM/HS], opened during the times and under the conditions considered appropriate by the Muslim Waqf and are not limited by time or certain circumstances, as expressed in your letter... The position of the Muslim Council and the Waqf in connection to the opening of the Hashmonean tunnel is clear. The matter will bring about an atmosphere of tension and dissatisfaction and will cause damage to the economy and to the city's image in the eyes of visitors from all over the world. Therefore, we demand that this tunnel not be opened.

The Minister for Public Security recommended to the Prime Minister to refrain from opening the exit to the tunnel during the month of Ramadan, especially since his representatives had not heard consent from the members of the Islamic establishment. The terror attacks by Hamas and the Islamic Jihad across Israel that followed the opening action did not allow an appropriate timing for opening the tunnel. As a result, the matter was postponed.[80]

Meanwhile, representatives of the Waqf received from the Israeli government (by means of police officials) tacit and informal agreement in principle to implement the work they initiated inside Solomon's Stables. The Jerusalem Municipality, within whose hands lies the authority as the local City Planning Committee, adopted its own policy. Its court for local affairs issued a decree of secession of works.[81] In response, Waqf representatives announced both publicly and in writing that they do not recognize Israel's authority to supervise work on the Haram, and they continued the work undisturbed.[82]

Building materials to the east of the Temple Mount (Photo: The Author, 2 February 2016)

Waqf leaders deliberately understated the scope of the work to be done, and it later turned out that the works were more extensive than what had been requested. Generally, verbal approval was granted, in principle, by Israeli government representatives to perform work on the Temple Mount. This translated into action by the police allowing entry of vehicles, equipment, and building supplies to the TM/HS in order to implement the work. The approval was given to keep up the system of arrangements, to encourage the Waqf to utilize an informal mechanism of communication and to maintain the status-quo. It could be that when the Israeli authorities gave their tacit approval, they thought they were merely discussing light work, but when that was not the case, they changed their position, but did nothing to stop the work. The Israeli police control the entrances to the TM/HS; Had the Israeli government or police wanted to prevent widespread construction projects, it could have forbidden the entrance of heavy equipment and building materials.

The unofficial deliberations between the police and the Waqf were hidden from the public for political reasons. The Israeli government could not admit publicly that it relinquished one of its sovereign powers—i.e., enforcement of the antiquities laws and construction on the Temple Mount. Once the broad dimension of the work was exposed for all to see, there was a public outcry on the Jewish side. A claim was filed with the court, demanding that the Israeli government enforce the supervision of the Antiquities Act, as well as the construction, planning and building laws, to restore the status-quo. The state responded to the court in several ways—all designed to obtain the court's backing for the government's policy: that the construction projects do not constitute a serious blow to the antiquities or to the laws of planning and construction; preliminary coordination took place on the matter; from now on the work will be closely monitored; and enforcement of the law could almost certainly lead to bloodshed.

Israeli government officials did not fully understand or expect the results of the Waqf's letter of negative reply regarding the Western Wall tunnel's opening. In any event, it appears no report of the Waqf's opposition was relayed to Benjamin Netanyahu's new government, (elected in June 1996), which decided to open the tunnel in September 1996. As mentioned previously, the Muslims saw the attempt to open the tunnel's exit, north of the Haram, as a violation of the status-quo and an attempt to Judaize this area.[83] Moreover, the Palestinians felt that Israel was plotting to establish an underground synagogue inside Solomon's Stables and thought that Israel's opposition to the building projects initiated by the Waqf did not derive from damage caused to antiquities, but from the elimination of the possibility of building a synagogue in that underground space.[84]

Opening of the egress to the Western Wall tunnel sparked widespread riots across the West Bank and Gaza Strip.[85] These riots exacted a steep bloody price, undermined the diplomatic process between Israel and the Palestinians and lead to a partial collapse of the arrangement of the post-1967 tacit understandings regarding the TM/HS.

The bloodshed that erupted in September 1996 in response to the opening of the Western Wall tunnel illustrated the heavy price Israel would have to pay if it was going to enforce Israeli law at Solomon's Stables, especially since government representatives gave a preliminary agreement, in principle, to the work projects on the site.

The impotency of the Israeli government's supervision and law enforcement stood out due to the fact that the Antiquities Authority and the Jerusalem Municipality—in charge of supervision and law enforcement—took pains to reduce the breadth of violations of the law to the Supreme Court, in stark contrast to their previous position. The Jerusalem Municipality's report stated that the Waqf did not commit any offenses, since the work projects were done in the internal space of Solomon's Stables which only constituted a change in designation. District archaeologist Gideon Avni said the renovations did not cause much damage.[86] After the municipality's legal advisor and its Director of Supervision toured Solomon's Stables under the protection of the police, it was reported that none of the work being carried out there violated the law, since the changes under discussion were solely internal. However, unofficial reports indicated that some of the work that had taken place did indeed break the law, and only due to constraints imposed by the political leadership, would it be reported to the court that the changes were only internal. Media reports stated that the Prime Minister instructed not to enforce the law, for fear of a renewal of riots.[87]

The work to prepare the Marwani prayer hall at Solomon's Stables was carried out with heavy mechanical equipment, and caused much damaged to the antiquities. Tons of earth that was dug out was poured into the Kidron Valley, into the Abu-Dis dump, and other places, without archaeological supervision, and apparently without the supervision of engineers.

In the year 2011, the State Comptroller completed a report on the enforcement of the laws regarding antiquities and construction on the TM/HS. The report was sent for review, but not circulated publicly, because the sub-committee on Security Affairs of the State Comptroller's Committee classified it as secret. Since the report was secret, it was not discussed in the State Comptroller's Committee and the public was unaware of the serious findings it contained. In 2014, the classified report was published on a New York Jewish news site (jewishvoiceny.com). From that moment, the report turned into a topic of conversation, especially among critics of government policy, and its contents became public knowledge.[88]

The State Comptroller's 2011 report points out deficiencies in supervision and in the obtaining of licenses to implement development projects on the TM/HS during the years 2001-2007: "Significant deficiencies were found in the performance of supervision, and in the manner which authorities dealt with enforcement of the law on the TM, when work took place without obtaining permits and approvals as required," as was case the with most of the work done in the years on which the report focused. The Marwani prayer hall was built without the authorities checking the necessary safety requirements for the Mosque—as it is a public building, the Mosque requires exits and entrances, equipment, devices and materials for extinguishing fires, fire alarms, emergency lighting and shelters. The Jerusalem Municipality's Department of Supervision sent a warning to the Waqf, but the Waqf director saw the warning, folded the paper and immediately returned it to the municipal inspector.[89]

In the report, the State Comptroller wrote, among other things, that until September 1996 the Antiquities Authority oversaw the activities of the Muslim Waqf on the TM. Its inspectors ascended the TM and toured it routinely, in order to detect any damage to antiquities. Inspectors were free to ascend the Mount, to enter every structure, and to record and photograph, without restriction and without police escort.

Following the opening of the Western Wall tunnel in September 1996, the Waqf administration announced to Israel's Antiquities

Authority "based on guidelines from above" it would halt the 'technical cooperation' between them. From now on, there would be no professional meetings between the parties, as had been in the past, and IAA inspectors would not be allowed to enter any closed structure on Al-Haram al-Sharif and inspect what was happening there. The State Comptroller determined that despite the state's commitment to reinstate the supervision, accompanied by police escort, "to date in 2011, supervision has not yet been renewed."[90]

The role of the State Comptroller is to verify the proper operation of the government according to state laws and the decisions of the supervising authorities. The Comptroller did not take into account that the government did not intend to implement the state laws regarding the Temple Mount and that even if it had wanted to do so, it was incapable of carrying out Israeli law on the TM/HS. It is possible that the Comptroller's report was archived and made confidential because it exposed the weakness of the state governing institutions.

After the renovation of Solomon's Stables was completed, the Waqf administration also began to prepare the level below the Al-Aqsa Mosque ('Al-Aqsa Al-Kadima') for prayer. Waqf officials asked Israeli police for a preliminary permit, solely to perform cleaning jobs on the site. This writer was on a tour of Al-Aqsa with students on the day these 'cleaning jobs' began, and was witness to the harsh public controversy that took place at the entrance to the Mosque between the police chief responsible for the TM/HS with his people and director of Al-Haram al-Sharif, Sheikh Muhammad Husayn.

Police representatives claimed that a permit was issued for cleaning work alone, not for removal of materials (the Waqf cleared away the remains of wooden Nur al-Din's *minbar*, burned in the mosque in 1969, to send them to be restored in Jordan). The discussion continued in the office of the Jerusalem District Waqf Director, Adnan al-Husayni, where it was agreed that the police approved cleaning jobs alone. Cleaning jobs quickly turned into a large-scale work project to prepare a prayer hall in the lower level of Al-Aqsa, including the opening of air vents. This prayer hall was inaugurated in 2001. Located in these halls are the Double Gate – the only passage that has been preserved intact from the Second Temple period, and led from the Western Hulda gate into the Temple Plaza. The work done included leveling rubble into the subterranean spaces, laying a new floor on an area of approximately 2,422 square meters, and the installation of lighting systems, with electrical pipes in the ground, including drilling into ancient stones.[91]

The works initiated by the Waqf did not end here. On August 9, 1999, the Waqf Administration opened a sealed window in the southwestern corner of lower level of the Al-Aqsa Mosque (in the corner of the Khatuniyya building, in the Southern Wall), in order to allow natural light and air into the prayer hall, and added metal guard bars and a security system. This act sparked concern among government officials that the actions of the Waqf were not intended merely to open a window and vent, but rather, a new entrance door to the TM/HS, from the direction of the excavation site in the southern portion of the TM/HS—which could possibly lead to Muslim control of the excavation site. This concern led to an urgent hearing in the office of the Minister of Public Security, resulting in the Minister advising the Prime Minister to see this as "a serious violation of the status-quo" and imposing upon police to seal the opening two-third height from the bottom portion.[92] Since in this case, the sealing work was done on the exterior side of the

TM/HS, the police were able to successfully enforce the decision without confronting the Muslim public within the complex. On the other hand, the possibility of enforcing the building ordinances and Antiquities laws on the TM/HS compound was discounted, for fear of riots and violence.

Entrance Steps to Al-Aqsa Al-Kadim (Photo: The Author, 2 February 2016)

In November 1999, the authorities gave the Waqf Administration permission, in principle, to open a small emergency opening to the prayer hall that was prepared in Solomon's Stables (Marwani prayer hall), provided that the work be coordinated with the Israel Antiquities Authority. For this purpose, police allowed the Waqf to bring vehicles and bulldozers onto the TM/HS. In practice, the Waqf Administration did not coordinate their work with Antiquities Authority (since the outbreak surrounding the northern entrance to the Western Wall tunnel in 1996, it was prevented from cooperating with the Israel Antiquities Authority), and took advantage of the agreement in principle to prepare a monumental opening, 12 meter wide, revealing three arches of the lower level, and to establish a large and wide staircase.

New entrance to the Marwani Hall (formerly known as Solomon's Stables) (Photo: Elad Melamed)

In fact, Waqf associates dug a vast pit of about 6,122 square meters wide and approximately 60 meters deep at the northern front of Solomon's Stables. The pit was dug with heavy mechanical tools and significantly damaged the earlier archaeological layers. The work led to the revelation of four ancient arched openings, approximately 4 meters wide and about 62 meters high, and they were stopped by Israel after two of the arches were opened. Over the course of the work project, excavators removed approximately 62,000 tons of rich earth amidst the archaeological findings. The Waqf disposed of that earth at the municipal garbage dump in Al-Ayzariyyah and other sites in East Jerusalem. After digging the pit, workers stabilized its side-walls with large and graded stones, built the framework for a monumental staircase, and prepared a wide plaza leading to the underground mosque, along whose sides they placed fancy lamp-posts and railings. The 'small emergency entrance' became the main passageway into the mosque.[93] If indeed approval was given only for a small opening to be created, the remainder of the work was done with the knowledge of the Israeli police, who facilitated the movement of heavy equipment to the TM/HS through the entrances under its control. It is more likely that government sources estimated in advance that these large-scale work projects were the subject being discussed. Nevertheless, the Israeli government chose to turn a blind eye to the work as part of its prevailing tacit understandings with the Waqf Administration.

When there was an outcry from various Jewish groups (movements of the Temple Mount, the Antiquities Authority, archaeologists, and intellectuals) the government ordered the police to prevent opening of the third arch. Although in the meantime, a large opening had already been opened across two of the original arches of Solomon's Stables. In the Temple Mount Faithful's petition filed with the Supreme Court demanding the return of the situation to what it had been, then state Attorney-General, Elyakim Rubinstein, declared that restitution of the situation "would, with a level of near certainty, lead to bloodshed, setting of fires, and excitement of passions, that will spill over from the Temple Mount to areas of Judea and Samaria and into the entire State of Israel." (The Attorney-General also ordered the authorities not to enforce the law on the TM/HS, except in consultation with him, and this, in light of the increased sensitivity involved.)[94] The Attorney-General's statement made it clear that enforcement of the Israeli Antiquities Laws and the Planning and Building Laws in the areas of the TM/HS exact a heavy toll, and the state must carefully weigh between enforcing the law and the price of possible bloodshed expected as a result. The Supreme Court accepted the state's argument and dismissed the petition.[95] The Court's decisions, pointing to the importance of political considerations in enforcement of the law on the TM/HS, resulted in decisions regarding if and when to enforce the law in this sensitive spot being made at the highest political levels based on the opinions of the State's Attorney-General, together with representatives of the defense establishment.

Enforcement of Israeli antiquities laws and building ordinances was restricted, as per the State's Attorney-General's 1987 guidelines, which relied on a Supreme Court ruling from 1968—according to which the situation on the TM/HS is "sensitive and filled with danger from the sectarian conflict." For years, the police had not been allowed to provide effective supervision over what was being done there, for fear of harming public safety.[96]

The police acted as an intermediary between the Waqf and the civil authorities, and in particular, the Antiquity Authorities and the Municipality.[97]

In April 2000, it was made possible for the Jerusalem region archaeologist to visit Al-Aqsa and Al-Kadima. However, his visit had a covert character and he was prohibited from photographing or filming the physical occurrences at the site.[98] The fact that the report submitted by the Antiquities Authority to the Court had been written by an archaeologist dressed in police uniform, unbeknownst to Waqf personnel, illustrates the dilemma of the Israeli government. It seems the government could not admit to the Court that it lacked any capacity to properly monitor the TM/HS and preferred to take this route. Moreover, the visit of the archaeologist in disguise was designed to help the State's representatives to reject the petition of the Temple Mount faithful, and to avoid the need to place Waqf personnel on trial for criminal charges for violation of the Antiquities Laws and Building and Planning Ordinances.[99] Ironically, the Israeli Government's Antiquities Authority, whom the Waqf did not permit to inspect at the TM/HS, went out of its way to cover up for the Waqf and assist it in breaking the law which it itself is responsible for enforcing.[100]

It should be noted that during the hearing of the petition regarding the work projects implemented by the Waqf in Solomon's Stables in 1996, and the construction of the new mosque, the Supreme Court commented as follows:

> No court in Israel requires proof that the excavation into the area of the Temple Mount by the Muslim Waqf, for the expansion of prayer space for

> Muslims, harmfully impacts the religious and national sensitivities of the broad Jewish public, regarding the most sacred place for Jews... Muslim expansion into another prayer area also affects the feelings of Jews toward the place ... This is one case in which a judicial decision is not a reasonable way to determine a dispute, and the resolution is beyond the limits of the law... it is the responsibility of the political echelon ... to give content and meaning to the historic cry: 'The Temple Mount is in our hands.'[101]

In other words, the Supreme Court authorized the executive branch to refrain from enforcing the law on the TM/HS due to political considerations. In January 2001, Jerusalem Mayor Ehud Olmert accused Prime Minister Ehud Barak of deciding not to enforce the law on the Temple Mount "purely for political reasons."[102] Due to the sensitivity of the matter, the Waqf was not obligated to submit requests for approval to the authorities, but merely reported to the police. Police then submitted the request to the State's Attorney-General. The Prime Minister was the one who authorized enforcement of the law on the TM/HS in those years.[103]

The above description reveals the ambiguous policy of the Israeli government. On the one hand, the government pretended to enforce the laws on the TM/HS, and on the other hand, it legitimized avoidance of its enforcement. As was the case of freedom of worship for Jews on the TM/HS, as well as the subject of the laws safeguarding antiquities, planning and construction, the fear of riots and potential

shedding of blood provided cause not to implement the law. In other words, the Muslims, who are a minority controlled by Israel, were able to successfully prevent the implementation of state laws on the TM/HS, in areas most critical to them, by using the threat of massive disruptions of the order.

In cases where the Waqf tried to implement work projects in the entrance to the Temple Mount—where the police have relatively easy control of the area—Israel successfully prevented the work projects from being implemented. For example, in 2000, the Waqf administration tried to replace the Mughrabi Gate, which was controlled by Israeli police.[104] This action was perceived as an attempt to existentially change the status-quo and was prevented from going forward by the police.

In summary

The large-scale work projects initiated by the Waqf, beginning in 1996 and the opening of the entrance to the Western Wall tunnels, caused a collapse of the covert understandings that had developed between the Waqf and the Israeli government after 1967, particularly in the areas of construction and maintenance of the laws regarding antiquities.

Access, Visitation, and Prayer

Following the violent events that erupted as a result of the opening of the Northern entrance of the Western Wall Tunnel's exit, administrators of the Waqf ceased coordinating their actions on the TM/HS with Israeli police and began dictating changes in the status-quo, not solely regarding the antiquities and construction. One change dictated by the Waqf was a unilateral decision to close the site to non-Muslim visitors, as happened in September 1996.

Attempts by Jewish ideological groups to increase opportunities for Jews to ascend to the Temple Mount, including pursuits to pray at the site, increased at the beginning of the 21st century. The exception was an official letter sent from Israel's Chief Rabbi Eliyahu Bakshi Doron to Prime Minister Ehud Barak in June 2000, on the eve of the peace talks between Israel and the Palestinians, sponsored by the United States at Camp David. In the letter, Rabbi Doron supported the Prime Minister, offering his approval not to insist on the rights of Jews to pray on the Temple Mount. In his letter, the Chief Rabbi recognized the status-quo regarding the Temple Mount, created after 1967, and called for Barak to safeguard it as a sacred arrangement for the future:

> It is our responsibility to respect and preserve the sacred status that exists regarding the Temple Mount, known to others as the area of the Al-Aqsa Mosque. We must act with suspicion concerning any change in the current status, as that would likely desecrate the sanctity of the space and lead to the spilling of blood, which every religion and every civilized society opposes. Rather than desecrating the sanctity of holy sites by fighting and endless debates, we must respect and accept the status-quo regarding all holy sites. We must work to secure access and security for everyone who wishes to participate in the ritual worship of these places that are sacred to him, according to his faith.[105]

This letter was harshly criticized by various political entities in Israel, causing the Chief Rabbinate to change its traditional position prohibiting Jews from entering the TM/HS. In August 2000, one member of the Rabbinate, Rabbi She'ar-Yashuv HaCohen (son-in-law of Rabbi Shlomo Goren, and an activist in inter-faith dialogue between Jews and Muslims), demanded that the Chief Rabbinate annul its decision prohibiting Jews from entering the Temple Mount, and plan to build a Jewish synagogue there. The Rabbinic Council did not accept his request. However, it did decide to establish a Rabbinic Committee "to examine every course of action to realize our rights and sovereignty over the Temple Mount."[106]

Later on, Rabbi HaCohen said: "Though unfortunately the de-facto situation is that the Palestinians and the Muslims control the Mount, to give that reality a seal of approval de-jure is simply a breach of trust given to us by the public, as the leaders of the generation. Whether referring to the government, or to the rabbinate, we must not give up on sovereignty over that place. This is our history. It is impossible to turn our backs on Jewish heritage."[107]

Knesset members from the National Religious Party *(HaMafdal)* pressured the Chief Rabbis to release a *hora'at sha'ah hilchatit* (temporary, ad hoc emergency legislation) to allow Jews to enter the TM/HS under the halachic definition of 'occupation.' (It was in this manner that they legitimized the presence of soldiers and policemen on the TM/HS during and after the Six Day War, ex post facto). The Chief Rabbis refused; however, the Council of the Chief Rabbinate issued the following decision:

> There is an absolute prohibition on the transfer of any authority or ownership of the Temple Mount—either directly or indirectly—to foreigners. The mere discussion of this topic is *Hilul HaShem,* blasphemy. The Chief Rabbinic Council stresses that the halachic issues preventing entrance onto the Temple Mount because of its inherent sanctity, do not detract in any way from our rights, our authority, or our ownership of the place that is the apple of our eye.

In its decision, the Council of the Rabbinate reminded Prime Minister Ehud Barak, once again, that he had promised not to give up any of Israel's holy sites.[108]

This is the place to acknowledge the contributions of the Jewish Temple activists, primarily from the religious-Zionist stream, to the erosion of the status-quo that crystallized after 1967. In order to understand the increasing tensions on TM/HS that reached a peak between fall 2014 and fall 2015, one must first take note of the increased Jewish-nationalist pilgrimages to this site, as a result of encouragement from rabbis of the centrist religious-Zionist stream and the actions of many supportive philanthropic organizations, both in Israel and worldwide. This activity was not lost on Muslims, who organized counter-measures, with the goal of making it difficult for Jews to visit the TM/HS and formulated a campaign of incitement, headlined, "Al-Aqsa is in Danger" (see below under the heading: demonstrations, symbols and flags).

These Jewish Temple advocate organizations launched a campaign for the reconstruction of a Third Temple on the site of the Dome of the Rock, believed to be the original spot where the Jewish First and Second Temples stood before their destruction and to reinstitute Jewish ritual worship at that location (see the illustration below). On September 15, 1998, the annual Conference of Temple Mount Advocates took place at *Binyanei HaUma* auditorium in Jerusalem, with thousands in attendance: religious-nationalists, haredim, and secularists. The rabbis at the conference instructed participants to begin practical preparations for the rebuilding of the Temple in place of the mosques. Invitations to the conference were sent by the Chairman of the Knesset's Constitution Committee, MK Hanan Porat, on official Knesset stationery. Porat also sent a recorded version of the greeting. At the conference MK Moshe Peled, Deputy Minister of Education at that time, also welcomed participants. In both a symbolic and concrete manner Knesset members and Israeli government officials had given their blessings to the plans of the Temple advocates. What had been the dream of an eccentric minority, just a few years earlier, become in time a legitimate aspiration within the religious-nationalist Zionist stream.[109]

In order to prepare for Jewish visitation to the TM/HS, first a halachic opinion was required to contradict the position of the Chief Rabbinate, which forbade entrance to the sacred site due to *'mora mikdash'* (the sanctity of the location). A significant halachic ruling permitting ascension to the Temple Mount was first released at the beginning of 1996, with the publication of the official letter on behalf of the Rabbinical Council of Ye"sha (Judea and Samaria). This ruling stated that going up to the Temple Mount was permitted and called on every rabbi who believed that visiting the Temple Mount was allowed "to ascend himself and instruct his congregants how to go, while adhering to all the halachic restrictions."

In his book *Jewish Fundamentalism and the Temple Mount*, Motti Inbari draws a connection between a weakening of the messianic paradigm that emanated from the Jewish settlement movement *Gush Emunim* and was deeply challenged by the Oslo Accords, with an intensification of the connection to the Temple Mount.[110] At the end of an extended process of persuasion the centrist stream of the religious-Zionist rabbis changed its position regarding visits to the Temple Mount and sided with the Temple Mount movement. In 2000, Rabbi Yisrael Ariel, the founder of the Temple Institute, published his position, permitting visitation to the Mount based on the commandment to conquer the land. It is an obligation to conquer (take over) every place in Israel, and therefore, it is permissible to enter these locations without limitation.[111] This position, adopted by Jewish Temple Mount advocates, marked an important turning point in the frequency of visitation by Jews at the site—since according to this ruling Jews were permitted to enter any place on the TM/HS and not just the southern section, considered to be a late extension from the Herodian era. In August 2000, a massive Jewish demonstration took place opposite the Lions' Gate, called "For the sake of the Temple Mount," in which approximately 50,000 people participated.[112]

In 2013, during a symposium conducted by the *'Ir Amim'* organization, Professor Haviva Pedaya (a liberal Haredi) spoke about the intensification of the interest in the Temple Mount amongst the religious-Zionist public. "The disengagement [from the Gaza Strip in 2005], for people who endured it, it was a kind of tearing away the tangible, from a point of connectedness … For the deportees, it was a breaking point that created a rift between the illusion and what was real—the land—symbolizing the State, the redemption." When this connection is severed, Pedaya explains, messianic hope was transferred to an alternative symbolic focus.

Hence, the Temple Mount replaced, among these groups, settlement of the Land of Israel as the key to salvation. It is possible that the disengagement contributed to the increased frequency of visits by Jewish religious-nationalists to the TM/HS, though this process began following the Oslo Accords (October 1993), because of a suspicion among these factions that the Israeli government might give up sovereignty over the TM/HS.

Another step in the process under discussion took place in 2007, when dozens of religious-Zionist rabbis visited the Temple Mount together. This visit reflected a change in the position of religious Zionism, which had previously been part of a broad halachic consensus shared by the Chief Rabbinate and the ultra-Orthodox world as well. The visit lasted two hours, in coordination with the Waqf and Jerusalem's police and was attended by representative religious-Zionist rabbis, including: Rabbi Dov Lior, Chair of the Rabbinic Council of Judea and Samaria; Rabbi Avi Gisser, Rabbi of Ofra; Rabbi Yaakov Medan, Head of the Yeshiva of Har Etzion; and Rabbi Aharon Harel, Head of the Shilo Hesder Yeshiva. Previously, four prominent mainstream religious-Zionist rabbis joined the cause—Yaakov Ariel, Haim Drukman, Avraham Zuckerman, and Tzefania Drori—adding in their signatures to the rabbinic proclamation permitting the entrance of Jews onto the

TM/HS compound.¹¹³ In June 2008, marking 40 years since the "unification of Jerusalem," 40 rabbis visited the Temple Mount, among them rabbis from Judea and Samaria, in order to challenge the position of the Chief Rabbinate.¹¹⁴

Rabbi Dov Lior with Haredi Rabbis on the Temple Mount.
(Photo: 'Temple Mount News' website)¹¹⁵

From the rabbinic arena, events moved to the political domain, with a union between rabbis and Knesset members. On July 27, 2009, the Knesset held a conference titled: "Jewish Sovereignty over the Temple Mount—Processes and Changes," organized by MK Michael Ben-Ari. Researcher and blogger Eran Tzidkiyahu, who was present at the conference reported:

> The public rose to their feet when Rabbi Yehudah Kreuzer, rabbi of the Mitzpeh Yericho settlement and head of the Yeshiva *HaRa'ayon HaYehudi* was called to the stage to talk about the importance of prayer on

the Temple Mount. The Temple Mount is the heavenly gate for Jewish prayer, to which all prayers flow on their way upward to heaven. Rabbi Kreuzer yearned for that short time after the war when Rabbi Shlomo Goren lead prayer services on the Temple Mount until he was forced to stop by his commanders. How is it that over the course of 42 years a simple ministerial decision prohibiting prayer on the Mount was not abolished, the wise rabbi innocently asked. The rabbi related that he and his students make sure to go up to the Mount each week. He told the story: after much deliberation regarding how we might succeed to pray on the Mount while accompanied by the Waqf and police, the barrier was broken accidentally on a hot summer day. One of Rabbi Kreuzer's followers said a blessing over water before he drank and caused a tremendous commotion on the Mount. The guardians of the Waqf started to scream that he was praying over the water. The police surrounded us quickly and started to remove us from the Mount. Is it forbidden to drink on the Mount? We were surprised. It's 'Forbidden,' the officer declared. At that moment, a group of tourists stopped to take a break to drink right near us. And this is how we took the advantage. Since that time, we always go up and make sure to recite a blessing over food and drink. The prayer for rain has been said and *Kaddish* has been recited on the Mount. Here, slowly, little-by-little, with stubborn persistence, prohibitions are broken and the Mount is conquered. In response to this story, the thrilled crowd stood as the Yeshiva leader came down from the stage.[116]

This process of legitimizing visits to the TM/HS is also reflected in the public opinion of the religious-Zionist community. In a survey conducted by 'Miskar' on May 18, 2014, within the religious-Zionist sector, 74.5% responded they were in favor of "Jews going up to the Temple Mount" and only 24.6% replied they were opposed. Additionally, 19.6% answered that they had already ascended the Mount, and 35.7% answered they had not yet gone up, but shared their intentions to do so in the future. In the above-mentioned survey, when the group of religious-Zionists was asked: "What are the reasons for the increase in Jews ascending the Temple Mount?"—98.6% of survey participants answered that going up to the Mount "contributed to strengthening Israeli sovereignty over the site of the Temple." Only 54.4% stated that ascending the Mount was "a positive commandment or they wished to go to fulfill a desire to pray (at this most holy site)."[117] Thus, national sentiment plays a more important role here than a halachic need among religious-Zionist respondents.[118]

Areas of the Temple Mount (color outlines based on image from Temple Mount News' website)[119]

In the early 1990s, there were only a few dozen religious Jews who entered the Temple Mount and encouraged others to do likewise. By the end of that decade that number had risen to 1,000 people.[120] Today, ascending the Temple Mount for religious and nationalist-political reasons has become a routine involving a large number of individuals and organizations that receive generous financial support.[121] In the year 2010, these organizations began to distribute 'Shabbat leaflets' at synagogues throughout Israel, specifying the dates on which the TM/HS was accessible and contact information on how to arrange a visit. They also established websites for that same purpose.[122]

What transpired on the Jewish side had a direct effect on the Waqf, Jordanian Authorities and the Palestinians. Any act that sought to make a change in the status-quo from the Jewish side was met with a counter-activity by the Muslims. For example, after the failure of the peace talks at Camp David II, an administrative decision was made by the Waqf, in August 2000, not to allow members of the Jewish Temple Mount Movement to enter Al-Haram al-Sharif. In response, Israeli government officials decided to use police control of the entrances to the Mount to prevent all tourists from entering, in order to harm Waqf revenues collected from entrance fees, until leaders of the Muslim establishment would choose to relent and reverse their decision. This measure turned out to be effective. A meeting between representatives of the two sides resulted in a return of the situation to its previous status.

Beginning from the events of October 28, 2000 and onward (that is, Ariel Sharon's visit and the outbreak of the

Al-Aqsa Intifada), the TM/HS was closed to visitors for three years, until August 2003, in keeping with the decision of Waqf Administrators. The Israeli government concealed the fact that the matter of visits to the TM/HS was already out of their control.[123] Only after Chairman of the Palestinian Authority Yasser Arafat was politically weak did security agencies under the direction of Minister of Public Security, MK Tzahi Hanegbi, manage to gradually and unilaterally resume non-Muslim visitation of the TM/HS—contrary to the Jordanian position. However, this did not include entrance into the upper and lower sections of Al-Aqsa Mosque, Dome of the Rock, Marwani Hall and the Islamic Museum. The Waqf Administration preferred to forfeit significant revenue from missed visitors' fees over the suspicion that fanatic Jewish elements might attempt to damage those buildings, and from a fear of reactions by fanatical Islamist elements. In addition, from time-to-time, Israeli police imposed age limits on the entry of Muslim men coming to Friday prayers and on days prone to disorderly conduct.

Demonstrations, Symbols and Flags

During the period between 1996-2003, Palestinian demonstrations over Al-Haram al-Sharif intensified, during which flags and political signs were used, and occasionally, the Israeli flag was burned in protest. For example, during the funeral and burial of Faisal al-Husayni at the edge of Al-Haram al-Sharif in 2001, huge Palestinian flags were waved in front of the Dome of the Rock and Al-Aqsa Mosque, as well as by the city wall at the Damascus Gate and the Muslim Quarter.[124]

The "Al-Aqsa is in Danger" Campaign of the Northern Islamic Movement

At the start of the 1990s, Sheikh Raed Salah, head of the Northern Islamic Movement and Mayor of the town of Umm al-Fahm at the time, began to interpret Israel's statements and actions as the harbingers of destruction of the Al-Aqsa Mosque. Public activities of the Jewish Temple Mount movements, statements made by senior Israeli officials regarding the Temple Mount, and various incidents that took place around the compound were intentionally inflated and constantly repeated in order to prove the existence of a real danger to the "Al-Aqsa site." It should be noted that any Israeli actions, oversights, and failures related to the TM/HS in any way creates a perception of danger on the part of Arab-Muslims even if no real threat exists. Nimrod Luz's research on ways discourse is structured among Arabs in Israel on the issue of Al-Haram al-Sharif shows that these messages have a major impact on non-religious Muslims and Christians as well. For example, MK Ahmad Tibi, who is not religious, believes Al-Aqsa is in danger "as long as it remains under foreign occupation."[125] Even though the claim that Israel is officially and continuously working to destroy Al-Aqsa is utterly baseless, it serves as a propaganda tool for political mobilization of the Arab Muslims. The construction operations in the 1990s on the underground level of the compound was a victory for Sheikh Raed Salah, when he built the Marwani prayer hall in the space of Solomon's Stables and prepared an additional prayer hall on the lower level of Al-Aqsa Mosque. These were seen as acts designed to curb Jewish intentions to build a synagogue in the lower level of the compound.

The Northern Islamic Movement's position is presented in a book about Jerusalem, in which Sheikh Raed Salah put forth his ideas. The book's introduction states that all Islamic holy sites are in danger, particularly Jerusalem and Al-Aqsa. The book's author, Yusuf al-Husayni, wrote that his research is intended to "expose the true face of the inhuman policy to destroy Islam's holy sites."

The claim that Al-Aqsa is in danger is fueled by Muslim commentators (innocently or maliciously), who view Zionism as a religious ideology with a goal of destroying Al-Aqsa Mosque and erecting a third Temple in its place.

The current scare-campaign, "Al-Aqsa is in Danger" bore more fruit than the actions of Haj Amin al-Husayni during the British Mandate period. It should be emphasized that the religious symbols of Al-Aqsa and Jerusalem and the propaganda associated with them do not stand on their own. They are part of a broader political struggle that includes the construction of myths and media propaganda. The "Al-Aqsa is in Danger" campaign integrates into the abundance of images and information that the Muslim world perceives about Israel and its actions in the Palestinian inhabited territories, and how Muslims worldwide view Israel. For example, Jordanian journalist Yasser Al-Za'atara wrote that although the television did not broadcast the festive convention of the Islamic Movement, 'Al-Aqsa is in Danger' (in 2002), it sufficiently spread throughout the entire Arab and Muslim world. Today, Al-Za'atara states, Sheikh Raed Salah is the main symbol of the Palestinian residents of the territories conquered since 1948—despite the fact the media ignores him.

The extent of the dissemination and impact of the message "Al-Aqsa is in Danger" can be understood from the fact that every year, the Islamic Movement in Israel announces its annual pan-Islamic essay contest published on their website, under the title *Jerusalem is in Danger.* In 2001, 20,000 essays were submitted, written by Muslims in 20 countries.[126] The movement also mobilized children and teenagers, in a conscious educational campaign, to collect donations in order to save Al-Aqsa. For example, on August 25, 2002, the Islamic Movement organized a major event named, "Fund for the children of Al-Aqsa" at the TM/HS compound. According to the organizers, 12,000 children were transported to the event, accompanied by their parents, in buses donated by Arab transportation companies. In an announcement made on behalf of the Islamic movement, the organizers were thanked along with the media outlets that covered the event, while Arab satellite stations were condemned for overlooking it. The movement expected to collect three million shekels in donations from the campaign, which was designated to pay for renovations of the compound.[127]

The 'Al-Aqsa is in Danger' political campaign reached its peak in 2013-2015, when the Islamic movement mobilized a group of men and women on the Haram whose job was "protection" of Al-Aqsa from the Jews. The *'murabitun'* (men defenders) and afterward, the *'murabitat'* (women defenders), surrounded and harassed the groups of religious Jews who went up to the TM/HS, screaming *'Allahu Akbar.'* They did not harass secular groups who visited the site, as I found on my visit there.

The police clashes with the *'murabitat'* precipitated the organization's being placed outside the law and caused dozens of its activists to be removed from the TM/HS, which inflamed tensions among Palestinians. The *'murabitat'* claimed credit for the outbreak of what they named "the al-Quds Intifada" in 2015.

Implications of the Peace Agreement between Israel and Jordan

The Peace Agreement between Israel and Jordan (1994) stipulated, among other things, that Israel respects Jordan's role in the oversight of Muslim holy sites in Jerusalem:

> 9 (2) In this regard, in accordance with the Washington Declaration, Israel respects the present special role of the Hashemite Kingdom of Jordan in Muslim Holy shrines in Jerusalem. When negotiations on the permanent status will take place, Israel will give high priority to the Jordanian historic role in these shrines.

The significance of this section is that a departure from the status-quo which preceded 1994 would be considered in the eyes of Jordan as a violation of the agreement, and such a violation could jeopardize the strategic alliance between the two countries and the peace agreement signed between them.

At the start of the 2000s, Israel approached Jordan with the request that Jordan intervene in the occurrences on the TM/HS in order to distance the Islamic Northern Movement from Al-Haram al-Sharif as much as possible. The activities of the Islamic movement posed a difficult challenge to the Israeli police. But Raed Salah was able to impose a sense of fear on Waqf officials. He published an article in his movement's journal, in which he demanded that Waqf officials refuse to admit Jews onto the Al-Aqsa compound. The "Al-Aqsa is in Danger" annual festival organized by Salah in the Umm al-Fahm stadium received mass participation among the Arab sector in Israel and its propaganda was distributed in many places throughout the Muslim world.

At the same time, the Israeli government faced an internal challenge brought upon by messianic and nationalistic Jewish elements and by public pressure groups designed to prevent damage to the archaeological and historical artifacts found on the TM/HS. This pressured the government to solve the problem of Jewish visitation to the site and to tighten the supervision over the activities of the Waqf.

Closer cooperation did begin, starting with a bulge that developed in the southern wall of the TM/HS during the second half of 2001. The Waqf and the Palestinian Authority opposed the repair being done by Israel's Antiquities Authority. Therefore, Israel's Prime Minister at the time, Ariel Sharon, decided to transfer the responsibility for implementing the necessary repairs to the Jordanian government, and it was they who ultimately took care of repairing the wall in 2003.

Since the local Waqf and Israel mutually opposed the other party attending to essential renovations, Israel welcomed the Jordanian government's willingness to do the job. This prevented setting a precedent of maintenance on the site being put in the hands of the Palestinians. Jordan was also requested to assist in restoring the routine that existed before September 2000, including the entrance of Jews and other visitors to the TM/HS. Jordan took advantage of the opportunity, and requested permission to build a fifth minaret on the eastern wall near the Dar-al-Quran structure, located near the Mercy Gate. While Israel rejected the request, it did not end the Hashemite regime's attempts to make its mark on the TM/HS.

Dar-al-Quran, close to the Mercy Gate (Photo by the author, 2 February 2016)

In 2015, the Jordanian Waqf received permission to improve the old entrance of Solomon's Stables (the space that already serves as a Marwani prayer hall) using a small elegant roof combined with glass. This work received the approval of Israel's Ministerial Committee for Jerusalem. However, when the work began, it quickly became evident that the project was rather ambitious and included a type of turret over the entrance. Therefore, Israel stopped the work, and the entrance remained covered in unsightly tin.

The old entrance to Solomon's Stables. In the background, children are playing in the open courtyard (Photo: author's collection)

As previously stated, Israel enabled Jordan to reconstruct the preacher's pulpit (*Nur al-Din's minbar*) that Saladin brought to the Al-Aqsa mosque—a platform that was nearly entirely burnt in August 1969, when a deranged Australian tourist hurled fire into the mosque. In 2007, Israel made it possible to return the restored *minbar*, that had been built anew under the auspices of the Hashemite Kingdom, to its place.

Repairing the restored Minbar in Al-Aqsa, February 2007 (Photo: author's collection)

Since 1967, Jordan has been involved in the on goings at Al-Haram al-Sharif, in the appointment of Waqf clerks and the funding of their salaries. Nevertheless, the 1994 peace agreement between Jordan and Israel, along with the invitation for Jordan's involvement in the overseeing renovations on the TM/HS, accorded Jordan an official status at the site. Since then, Israel has been forced to respect the opinions of Jordan in various matters concerning the TM/HS and its surrounding compound. Thus, for example, in February 2007, when Israel began the dismantling of the Mughrabi Ramp in order to build a bridge in its place, Abdullah II King of Jordan harshly criticized the action. According to his claim, this work caused disturbing tension that would likely harm the renewal of dialogue between Israel and the Palestinian Authority (and in any case, harm relations with Jordan, Y.R.).[128] In light of this situation, Israel froze its plan to build the bridge, meant to replace the old ramp, as well as the construction of the temporary wooden bridge intended to replace the existing wooden bridge.[129] In recent years, coordinating-meetings have been held between the Israeli police and senior Jordanian government officials regarding the TM/HS every three to four weeks. In these meetings the two groups coordinated issues related to the management of the site, matters of security, and public safety at the site. Both sides are working to weaken the involvement of Hamas and the Northern Islamic Movement in the compound.

In conclusion
In September 1996, the modus-vivendi that had existed on the TM/HS since 1967 collapsed (and hence, so did the status-quo),

It had been created by tacit understandings between authorities in Israel and the Waqf administration, which reported to the Jordanian government. These understandings were accepted with bitterness by the Palestinian Authority and incessant pressure from the Northern Branch of the Islamic Movement in Israel. Collapse of the shared understandings led to a brief unilateral closing of the TM/HS to visits by Jews in 1996, and again in September 2000. Following the protest visit of Ariel Sharon to the site (to be discussed in the next chapter), the TM/HS was closed for three years. In addition, the Waqf carried out extensive work on the TM/HS without building permits and without allowing the Israeli Antiquities Authority to supervise what was being done at that location.

CHAPTER 7
Erosion of the Status-Quo and Creation of New Conditions Forged by Israel, 2003–2015

In fall 2000, at the climax of the discussions between Israel with the Palestinians on the sovereignty over East Jerusalem and the Old City, the question of who controls the TM/HS became a practical question. The September 28, 2000 visit of Likud Chairman and Opposition Leader at the time Ariel Sharon to the Temple Mount, together with six additional Likud Knesset members and accompanied by a large security force, was the trigger for the outbreak of the second Intifada—and the impetus behind naming it with a term that gave it religious significance: The Al-Aqsa Intifada. Sharon's visit was seen as defiance and an attempt to prove Israel's sovereignty over the Temple Mount.

In a report submitted by the Israeli Government to the International Mitchell Commission, which examined the circumstances behind the conflict in the Palestinian territories, it was written, "The prospect of banning the visit [by Sharon] was considered. However, freedom of access to holy sites is stipulated by Israeli law and by the ruling of the Supreme Court. In addition, the freedom of movement of Knesset members is secured by Israel's law, and therefore, the ability to constrain a member of Knesset's movement was limited."[130] However, if Israeli Prime Minister Ehud Barak had wanted, he could have prevented the demonstrative visit by basing his decision on precedents backed by Supreme Court rulings.[131] It appears that Barak believed that preventing Sharon's visit would be interpreted by the public as conceding Israeli sovereignty over the TM/HS, and would weaken his political standing within Israel as well as in negotiations with the Palestinians. His decision was aided by intelligence reports and on assessments of the Palestinian security apparatus, along with a senior Palestinian public figure, who claimed that if Sharon would arrive in the early morning hours and not enter the mosques, there would be no widespread disturbances.[132] Ex post facto, it turned out that Israel's sovereignty was put to the test as a result of this visit—which actually led to the weakening of Israel's standing in its dispute with the Palestinians and regarding the TM/HS.

The Muslim mass demonstration after Friday prayers at Al-Haram al-Sharif, the day after Sharon's visit, led to a harsh confrontation with police forces, who entered the Mount and opened fire on the rioters, fanning the flames that broke out afterward. Israeli officials assumed that riots were likely to break out in the territories, in any case, either as part of a strategy outlined by the head of the Palestinian Authority at that time, Yasser Arafat, or as a spontaneous action of the Palestinian public. However, in light of the extreme sensitivity regarding Al-Aqsa in the eyes of Muslims, Sharon's visit to the TM/HS added religious fuel to the fire of conflict and resulted in its rapid expansion to additional internal and external fronts. What began as spontaneous resistance by the Waqf administrators, the Muslims in Jerusalem, and the Arab Knesset members (who protested on the TM/HS at the time of Sharon's visit),[133] along with nearly 1,000 rioting

Muslims on the TM/HS during Sharon's visit and over the course of the following day (30 police officers were wounded, among them, the Jerusalem district commander and ten Palestinians)— became quickly taken advantage of by the Palestinian Authority, who encouraged acts of violence for political purposes. The PA primarily sought to strengthen its political position in advance of the upcoming round of negotiations, and alternatively, toward proclaiming a unilateral declaration of a Palestinian state, with its capital in East Jerusalem.

The Al-Aqsa Intifada began in the territories of the Palestinian Authority, on the same scope as the 1996 riots, when the Palestinian police and political organizations participated in the shootings of Israelis. However, the events this time, in an unprecedented manner, swept up Arab-Israeli citizens, as well as various populations throughout the Muslim world.[134] Even if Sharon's visit to the TM/HS had been just an excuse for the outbreak of riots, his visit contributed to Israel's weakened standing with regard to sovereignty over the Temple Mount. Muslim resistance to this visit was seen in full force, and it became clear what heavy price would be exacted from Israel over any attempt to exercise sovereignty over the site.

One week after Sharon's visit, Palestinian officials declared a "Day of Rage" (October 6, 2000), and for the first time, Israeli police relinquished their presence on the TM/HS and placed responsibility for security checks in the hands of the Waqf guards and security personnel of the Palestinian Authority.[135] Palestinian demonstrators took over the police station inside the TM/HS, set it on fire and forced the evacuation of worshipers from the Western Wall Plaza. This proved again that Israel's claim of sovereignty over the TM/HS was weak.[136] The essence of the coordination with Palestinian security forces revealed the fact that even in the area of security, Israel had conceded sole sovereign authority over the site.

We should explain here the meaning of the term 'sovereign,' in comparison to words such as 'ownership', 'control' and 'administration' of the TM/HS. 'Sovereignty,' in international law, is the authority of a country to employ force in some geographic area, or over a specified group of people. This authority is accorded to the country by virtue of their constitution, legal institutions or international agreements. On June 1967, Israel began applying its laws and administration in East Jerusalem, including the TM/HS. This means that the laws of the State of Israel should be applied to areas of the Temple Mount/Al-Haram al-Sharif. To the extent that these laws were challenged and not enforceable, as is indicated in this essay, indeed, the alleged sovereignty of Israel has not been fully realized. To describe the authority of Israel over the TM/HS (particularly regarding issues of security and the ability to employ force), perhaps one should use the term 'control.' It is possible to use the term 'administration' to describe the role of the Waqf on the TM/HS (in determining the order of worship, behavior and management). Yet widespread use of the term 'sovereignty' in Israeli political discourse also carries symbolic meaning. When Israelis say: 'We lost our sovereignty' or 'we have no sovereignty,' they actually are saying that their claim to sovereignty is a presumption that cannot be implemented or cannot be implemented willingly.[137]

Police and Israeli government officials are of the opinion that since 2003 Israel has been exercising sovereignty over the TM/HS by virtue of being a military and police force, enabling it to enforce its will. Abandoned police stations on the TM/HS, particularly during sensitive periods, refraining from inserting police on the TM/HS during the four Fridays of the month of Ramadan and other sensitive times, failure to enforce Jewish freedom of worship, a lack of full enforcement of the laws of construction and antiquities—all these appeared to those same responsible bodies like calculated, one-time concessions alone. On the other hand, it is possible to claim that Israel's sovereignty over the Temple Mount was only partial, and reflects a voluntary concession of the full realization, from an informed approach and from a realistic political point of view.

A tangible expression of the complicated situation can be found in the words of Israel's police commander of the Jerusalem district at the time, Police Chief Mickey Levy, who was asked by an Israel television reporter: "Why didn't the police prevent the violent demonstration on the Temple Mount, during which the police station next to the Lions' Gate was set ablaze?" Levy answered: "There is no problem preventing such an attack. The question is at what price? If I had given the order to prevent it (the demonstration)—the price would have been heavy."[138] The Minister for Public Security, Shlomo Ben-Ami, said in the same context, in an interview with Galei Zahal, army radio: "More than we are sovereign over the Temple Mount, today we are Temple Mount hostages."[139] It appeared that in order to realize Israel's aspirations of sovereignty over the TM/HS and the surrounding compound, the state was forced to pay a heavy price, politically and in terms of security.

Management and maintenance
remained in the hands of the Waqf during this period, as it had been before. Maintenance work required permits and approvals, which were given sparingly.

Access, visitation and prayer
Since Ariel Sharon's visit to the TM/HS at the end of September 2000, the Waqf administration closed the TM/HS to non-Muslim visitors and decreased their cooperation and coordination with the Israeli police. In the summer of 2003, an agreement was signed between the commander of the Jerusalem police district, headed by Police Chief Mickey Levy, and the administrators of the Waqf on the TM/HS regarding the reopening the site to visitors. The agreement was signed on behalf of the Waqf, by Eng. Abd al-Azim Sahlab, chairman of the Waqf Committee; Adnan al-Husayni, director of the Waqf in Jerusalem; Sheikh Muhammad Husayn, director of the mosques, and the Mufti of Jerusalem. The people of the Waqf requested the permission of the Chairman of the Palestinian Authority for this agreement. Yasser Arafat met the Waqf leadership on July 23, 2003, after he consulted with Sheikh Taysir al-Tamimi, and expressed his opposition to the agreement. Taking that into account, Waqf officials reneged on the agreement.[140] Hence, Israeli police forced the visitation of non-Muslims unilaterally.

The number of Jews visiting the TM/HS had been relatively low: approximately 11,000-12,000 per year, and to date, does not reflect the potential number of visitors, in light of the support of the rabbis and other entities who favor ascending the Mount.

Jewish visitors to the TM/HS can be divided into five categories, based on the purpose behind their visit:

- **Regular tourists** (mostly secular or traditional) whose visit is not specifically intended as a religious experience;
- **Religious tourists** whose visit is primarily intended to realize a religious experience, though they do not identify with the actions of the Temple Advocate movements;
- **Visitors whose motives are both nationalist and religious alike**, mostly from within the ranks of religious-Zionists, and whose religious experience is part and parcel of the nationalist experience that carries a hope for the realization of Jewish sovereignty over the Temple Mount. These visitors seek to pray at the site and hope to build a synagogue or Jewish prayer area at the site;
- **Ideological non-religious visitors** from 'Im Tirzu' ('If you will it') or similar groups, i.e., Students for the Temple Mount, whose interests are nationalistic;
- **Religious visitors who belong to the Temple Movements,** whose vision calls for building a Third Temple, in the place where the Dome of the Rock currently stands.

The last three groups are ideological and seek to change the status-quo at the TM/HS site from a nationalist viewpoint—

meaning the realization of full sovereignty, including control and management of the Temple Mount site by the Jews. From their perspective, Jewish prayer on the Temple Mount is a matter of national pride. The last two groups are also motivated by religious emotion—a longing to reinstitute Jewish worship at the Temple Mount and to restore its former Israelite glory.

The ideological groups arrive at the Temple Mount mostly on holidays and festivals (especially during the holidays in Nissan and Tishrei), or on other days when large numbers of Jews come together. On regular weekdays, 20-30 visitors come to the TM/HS and 150-300 visitors on holidays. Among the visitors there are those who recite prayers disguised as a phone call, or a conversation with themselves. Sometimes, they bow toward the place where the Holy of Holies was likely located in the Temple.

During the years 2003-2012, the police imposed severe restrictions on Jewish ideological groups visiting the TM/HS. In order to reduce friction with the Waqf and Muslim worshippers, the police customarily acted to curtail the steps of Jewish zealot groups in different ways. In the past, police allowed Jews whose motives for visiting were ideological or ritual (as opposed to regular tourists), to enter the compound in pairs or trios, entering on a path distanced from the mosque and the Dome of the Rock, with police escorts, carrying video cameras and accompanied by guards on behalf of the Waqf. The intense inspection of their equipment and belongings lasted quite some time, which prevented many of them from entering the site before it closed. Maintaining a quota limiting the number of Jewish ideological visitors enabled the police and the Waqf to ensure they carefully adhered to the rules—ensuring that visitors were not praying either openly or secretly, and that they were not bringing in religious articles, prayer books, or pictures of the Temple with them.

Chief Avi Biton, former police commander of the TM/HS and Chief of the David sub-district, framed the task of the police in this context: "A Jew who is clearly religious, who ascends to the Temple Mount, creates a double threat with his ascent. On the one hand, there is the threat directed at him by Muslim extremists. On the other hand, there is the threat the Jew himself could create vis-à-vis the place, should he violate the rules of his visit. There are days that the tensions are high and the security team at my disposal is only sufficient to bring a group of two to three Jews, while the rest remain outside."[141]

It appears that the working assumption of the police—i.e., that danger to the public order is present every day on the TM/HS—has changed recently, since the police have occasionally allowed groups of the Temple Mount Faithful to ascend in larger numbers, while successfully protecting their safety. In the second decade of the 2000s, the police enabled an increase in the number of people entering the TM/HS in a group to 50.[142] In the past, the Waqf could veto the entrance of 'troublemakers'—Jews caught violating the accepted rules. However, this cooperation stopped, and from August 2003, the Israeli police had exclusive jurisdiction over these issues. Determining the size and pace of the incoming visiting groups is no longer under the control of the Jordanian Waqf, and as a result, these parameters have since been set by the Israeli authorities. According to the Waqf, this change prevented its guards from properly supervising visitors, and made them—as well as the Jordanians—into powerless entities in the eyes of the Muslim public. Some of the

Jewish religious groups arrived with rabbis, clearly identifiable as 'ideological' groups, which in the eyes of the Muslims expressed a desire to confiscate Al-Haram al-Sharif from them and turn it into a Jewish Temple; or alternatively, to divide the holy site into two, similar to Israel's control of the Cave of the Patriarchs in Hebron.

Ideological visits to the TM/HS have escalated over recent years and peaked in 2014, when terrorist attacks broke out in East Jerusalem—among them, in protest over the situation in 'Al-Aqsa.' The escalation occurred when political figures, ministers and Knesset members regularly took part in the ritual of visiting the Temple Mount. At the end of 2012, ads were printed in Israeli newspapers that called for "the cleansing of the Temple Mount from enemies of Israel." These ads caused unrest in East Jerusalem, after which police decided to prevent Likud member/ Deputy Chairman of the Knesset, MK Moshe Feiglin (who denied any connection to the above-mentioned ads) and his supporters from entering the site. They also closed the TM/HS to non-Muslim visitors, because of a fear of disturbing the peace.[143]

As more politicians who support the right of Jews to visit and pray on the Temple Mount joined the government and the Knesset, both implicit and explicit political pressure was exerted on police to facilitate entry of Jews into the site. If that were not the case, then it would be difficult to understand how it happened that during three tense days of the holiday Rosh Hashanah on September 13, 2015, police allowed 650 Jews to visit the Temple Mount, and for that purpose, they even burst into the Al-Aqsa Mosque in the early morning hours to arrest Muslim youth who had barricaded themselves inside Al-Aqsa with stones and other assault tools.[144]

Muslim youth barricaded inside door 7 (the Eastern-most) of Al-Aqsa Mosque (Author's collection)

Door 7: The Eastern-most door of Al-Aqsa Mosque during calm times (Photo by Author 2 February 2016)

Moreover, Minister Uri Ariel was among those who entered the Temple Mount (contrary to the assurances Israeli authorities provided King Abdullah in November 2014), stood at the steps below the Dome of the Rock and was documented reciting 'Birkat HaKohanim,' the Priestly Blessing, directly in opposition to understandings of the status-quo. To make matters worse, the video clip of this occasion was distributed publicly. In September 2015, the TM/HS first opened to Jewish visitors on Yom Kippur and 37 Temple Mount supporters visited there. In addition, approximately 60 Jews crowded into a synagogue in the Mahkama building for Yom Kippur services. According to the website Temple News, "half of the synagogue was built on the Temple Mount, and it is treated with the sanctity of the Temple Mount, including the recitation of prayers and blessings in the version that applies to the Temple Mount, along with bowing and outstretched hands and legs."[145]

The Temple Institute, located in the Jewish Quarter, educates toward the resumption of the construction of the Jewish Temple and the ritual practiced there. The government of Israel supports this institute primarily by directing students to it. A film that is screened at this institute presents replacing the Dome of the Rock with the Third Temple and asks viewers: "What are each of you doing to achieve the realization of this vision?" In the institute's publication, Prime Minister Benjamin Netanyahu is shown shaking the hand of Yehuda Glick, one of the most prominent activists on behalf of the Temple Mount.

In the years 2013-2014, nearly half of all Likud party Knesset members took actions in attempts to enable Jews to ascend the

Temple Mount, including several secular members. Government ministers and deputy-ministers ascended to the Temple Mount in increasing numbers, making sure they went to the upper-platform of the Dome of the Rock—a place Jewish Temple advocates previously avoided treading, owing to their reverence for the Temple. Deputy-Minister Gila Gamliel stated: "The Temple Mount is the identity card of the Jewish people," and MK Yariv Levine referred to the Temple Mount as 'the heart of the nation.' Yehudah Glick, the man who coined that phrase, was elected in 2015 to the 33rd spot on the Likud list for Knesset, and in May 2016, began serving in the Knesset. Moreover, Deputy Foreign Minister Tzipi Hotovely shared in an interview on the Knesset TV channel that her dream was to see an Israeli flag flying over the Temple Mount. Hotovely's statement came after Netanyahu reached agreements with the King of Jordan, mediated by U.S. Secretary of State, John Kerry, regarding preventative measures against Temple Mount agitators following the 'Al-Aqsa crisis' that erupted in October 2015. In response, Netanyahu ordered Hotovely to cancel her press briefing with foreign journalists.[146] It should be noted that Netanyahu did not take similar actions before tensed situation.

    MK Miri Regev exerted pressure on the police while she chaired the Internal Affairs and Environmental Protection Committee of the Knesset during the years 2013-2014. She held 15 meetings on the subject of Jews ascending to the Temple Mount, during which she continually criticized the police for not enabling more Jews to ascend the Mount. Thus, for example, Regev said in one of the discussions: "I ask the police to prepare itself for Jews praying [at the Temple Mount] during the Jewish high holidays." Regev added: "If you do not succeed [in preparing], let's give responsibility over [security on] the Temple Mount to the IDF."[147] Former police commander of the Jerusalem District, Chief Yossi Pariente, stated on television that the intense and obsessive preoccupation of the Knesset Interior Committee regarding this issue caused great unrest in the Muslim World and gave a boost to many Jewish organizations who have their eyes set on the Temple Mount.[148] It should be noted that many activists from these organizations participated in the Knesset committee's discussions while Israeli Arab MKs took part in the discussion as well.

The situation on the Temple Mount began to escalate during the Jerusalem Day celebrations in 2013. It appears that the cause of the increased tension was the proposal of Deputy Minister of Religious Affairs, Rabbi Eliyahu Ben Dahan, to enact regulations that would provide for an increase in the number of Jews accessing the Temple Mount and allowing Jewish prayer on the Mount. On May 8, 2013, MK Miri Regev, who was then Chair of the Knesset Interior Committee, conducted a festive gathering of the committee to mark Jerusalem Day, at which she presented Ben-Dahan's recommendations. That same day, Minister Uri Ariel went to pray on the Temple Mount (as he did again on September 11, 2013). A senior police official believed these events caused Muslims to fear that Israel intended to take over Al-Aqsa Mosque. Seeing a minister enter the TM/HS with a security escort breaches the status-quo (and evidence of that violation was uploaded to YouTube). Muslims protested the violation and soon, a group of Morabitat began harassing Jewish visitors.

Minister Uri Ariel blesses Rabbi Zalman Kalmanovitz at the Temple Mount on September 22, 2013. (From the 'Temple Mount News' website)[149]

On July 15, 2013, Rabbi Ben-Dahan spoke at a rally, at the conclusion of the Tisha B'Av march held near the Lion's Gate—which was a symbolic location, thanks to the IDF paratroopers unit who captured the Temple Mount—and revealed that his ministry was preparing regulations that would allow [Jewish] prayer on the TM/HS. Rabbi Ben-Dahan added: "The time has come to return control of the Temple Mount to our hands."[150]

In February 2014, in one of the meetings of the Knesset Interior and Environmental Protection Committee, a sub-committee to address the subject of "ascension of Jews to the Temple Mount" was appointed, in response to committee chair MK Miri Regev's request to implement the government's decision to allow the ascension of Jews to the Temple Mount. The sub-committee was composed of retired Commander MK David Tzur (*HaTnua*), MK

Nachman Shai (Labor) and MK Zevulum Kalfa (*HaBayit HaYehudi*). Not a single Arab Knesset member participated in these sub-committee discussions. The committee presented its main findings to the Interior Committee on June 23, 2014, less than three months before the events of September 2014 erupted, for which the matter of the TM/HS was one of the accelerants. The sub-committee report was not published. However, from David Tzur's summary presented to the Interior Committee plenum, it is possible to learn about the way in which the Israeli establishment understands the status-quo and the changes it wants to implement.[151] The Arab Knesset members who were active on the subject of Al-Haram al-Sharif also participated in the plenum discussion and hence learned and disseminated the information regarding how the Israeli side interpreted the status-quo and intended to change it.

The interpretation of the 'status-quo' presented by the sub-committee was that the 1967 status quo continues; however, MK David Tzur himself stated the opposite: "after the Temple Mount was closed due to riots in October 2000, in 2003 it was opened [emphasis added] to the status-quo that had been in place since 1967. A portion of these changes constitute a deterioration, and some of them an improvement, it depends: everyone views it from his own perspective."

This is how MK Tzur described the "status-quo" of 2014:

What actually became a permanent part of the status-quo upon which our operating procedure is based today? Today, Jews and tourists ascend the Mount on Monday-Thursday. This is executed through the

Mughrabi Gate, between the hours of 7:30am-11am and from 1:30pm-2:30pm in the summer, with the break in-between visiting hours set for the purpose of holding Muslim afternoon prayers on the Mount. During the winter season, visitation hours are shorter, from 7:30am-10:00am and 12:30pm-1:30pm. Jewish prayer is not permitted on the Mount. There is a new understanding between the police and the Waqf to restrict the entrance of ideological visitors to a maximum of 60 people. Police escort visitors up in groups of 25-30 people, one group at a time. When one group finishes, the second group would enter. Those interested in praying were directed to the Western Wall. Management of the Mount and the religious endowments have been administered by the Waqf since 1967.

The Jordanian government holds a special status, in accordance with the peace agreement signed in 1994. Entrance gates to the Mount are manned by the Waqf, while Israeli police are responsible for the security. This is what was established shortly after 1967, when, following a government decision, the military forces were pulled out. The sub-committee laid out its independent findings: The status-quo continues from 1967. Everything related to visitation times and ascension of Jews to the Mount has been preserved. The Israeli police are the ones responsible for carrying out the government's policies ... regarding the quantity of visitors. We recognize that the quantity of visitors to the Mount is trending upward—with regard to both tourists and Jews who are going up to the Mount. We

> are talking about approximately 280,000 tourists, amongst whom 9,000 are Israelis ... It is important to note that lately visitors have included soldiers in uniform—approximately 2,000 per year. This generally happened in an organized manner, the wait on lines could last as long as two or three hours ... Whoever does not succeed in entering in this time frame will come a different day ... incidentally, most of them are tourists ... The number of incidents in which the Mount is closed [to Jewish visitors], following the disorderly conduct which is constantly on the rise ... The instances in which the police employed the method of restrictive access, i.e., banning Muslims under age 50 from entering; and measures setting an even higher threshold are on the rise, as part of a process in which the police are trying to control the crowd and reduce the number of riots. The number of times police find it necessary to storm the Mount in order to restore order has gone up significantly. There is a clear correlation between increased invasions and the number of disturbances of the peace...

Proposals of the sub-committee, as presented by Tzur, included, among others:

> The committee proposes preservation of the status-quo. We do not believe it is necessary to take legislative action to change the status-quo from 1967, we just think it needs to be better implemented. The existing erosion of the status-quo needs to be reversed. This statement refers to the desire to be

> open to the practice of [Jewish] religious ritual, to prayer or to establishing some arrangement, as there had been ideas for organizing prayer at the Cave of the Patriarchs, for both Jews and Muslims. We do not think it is necessary to open discussion on the topic ... We think it is necessary to strengthen moderate factions, to maintain the Jordanian channel which has a special status in accordance with the peace agreement, and to strengthen the Waqf.

Despite the proposals of the sub-committee calling for implementation of the 1967 status-quo, they suggested including several changes: Closing of the TM/HS to all visitors (including Muslim worshippers) in extreme cases of disruption of the order; opening of the TM/HS to visitors on the Jewish Sabbath as well; the addition of checkpoints on the way up from the Mughrabi Gate (so that more Jews and tourists would be able to enter through it); and encouragement of the Waqf to collect entrance fees to the Dome of the Rock, as an incentive to maintain order.

Former Commander of the Jerusalem District, and then-Police Chief, Yossi Pariente, said the following at the same meeting, indicative of the condition of the situation at the site:

> It is important to note that in 2014 there is an increase in the quantity of Jews ascending the Temple Mount. There has been a 27% rise in the number of Jews going up to the Temple Mount compared to the same period last year. In 2014, the police of the Jerusalem District were forced to breach the Temple Mount eight times in five months [the first months of the year]—This

refers to entries that were just mentioned here, which include the use of force, in order to impose order on the Temple Mount, in comparison to eight times over the course of the entire year of 2013. It was necessary to implement restrictions on access of Muslims to the Temple Mount 16 times … Some of these access restrictions took place on Fridays. On Fridays, 35,000 [Muslim] ascend the Temple Mount to pray. When we implement access restrictions, no more than 5,000 Muslims enter. Each Friday on which we impose access restrictions, approximately 30,000 Muslims are banned from entering the Temple Mount because of the policy of restrictions. That refers to Fridays. I can also give examples from the recent holidays. When we have intelligence information that attempts are being made to prevent the ascension of Jews, then we take preliminary measures, including restricting access. We prevent the ascension of Muslims of specific ages, who are generally the same group who riot, in order to ensure that Jews, visitors, and tourists will be able to enter the Temple Mount. In 2014, we were forced to partially close the Temple Mount site [to Jewish visitors] six times. A full closure lasts a full day, meaning cancellation of both morning and afternoon visitation. Partial closure means we close the site in the morning, or the afternoon, or when Jews entered during the first hour and riots began. These are examples of partial closings … when Jewish visitation begins on the Temple Mount and riots with stone throwing and firecrackers commence, and the police need to burst in, it is impossible to continue routine visitation ... The Temple Mount is also closed to Muslims. We can describe a number of instances in which we closed the Mount to Muslims as well.

Pariente said that the Jerusalem District believes the proposals of the sub-committee are the necessary recommendations. Then Police Chief, Yochanan Danino, emphasized in that same meeting that when police restrict the age of Muslims permitted to enter Al-Haram al-Sharif (an action referred to as 'restrictive access'), they must allocate 4,000 police officers to ensure public order, and Danino added:

> There are situations in which we brought thousands of police officers one day prior, in order to restrict access of Muslims and to enable Jews to ascend. Do you know how many police officers I sent up to Jerusalem as a result of the 120 Jews who ascended; how much money the State spent in order for these police officers to secure the entrance of Jews to the Mount? ... I am telling you, I am extremely dissatisfied with every incident in which we are forced to storm the Mount. Why are we infiltrating the Temple Mount? We are infiltrating the Temple Mount in order to secure the welfare of those praying at the Western Wall. There are thousands who come there and pray. You want them to return home in peace, you do not want the rocks they [Muslim rioters] throw to reach them.

Yehuda Glick, Chair of the Temple Mount Heritage Fund, stated in the meeting that a division of time must be reached to establish separate visiting hours at the Temple Mount, during which Muslims will not be able to visit, and in this context, he mentioned the separation customary at the Cave of the Patriarchs.

At the same meeting Arab MK Ahmad Tibi presented the complaints from the Muslim perspective:

> Recently, there is a kind of creeping change in the status-quo taking place. A) More and more of the gates of the mosques and the area of the compound are being closed to Muslims. They are being closed for more days. For every minor incident, they [police] close it for a few hours, for a day, and the like, after which they allow access to Jews and politicians whose objective is to provoke and to incite.

Committee Chair, MK Miri Regev, relayed that she requested that the police enable Jews to visit the Temple Mount during Jewish holidays like Sukkot, Shavuot, and Chanukah: "On Shavuot, and on Sukkot, I begged the Police District Commander, please, these are Jewish holidays. Let them ascend."[152] MK Regev said she asked for permission for all the members of the Knesset Interior and Environment Protection Committee to visit the Temple Mount. However, her request was rejected by the police.

All in all, the discussions of the Knesset's Interior Committee show an erosion of the 1967 status-quo. This is reflected in some significant ways, which are at the center of the controversy that incites violence:

- A rise in the number of Jews visiting, and among them, wearers of IDF uniforms;
- Closing of the TM/HS, from time-to-time, to Jewish visitation, or to Muslim prayer, including restricted entrance during Friday prayers based on age;
- An escalation in the number of disturbances by Muslims and more frequent intrusions of the police onto the TM/HS compound in order to secure the welfare of Jewish worshippers at the Western Wall, as well as ensuring the possibility for Jews to visit the TM/HS;
- An increase in the cost of security to protect Jewish visitors and maintain public order on the TM/HS.

In addition, raising the discussion regarding the division of visitation times on the TM/HS between Jews and Muslims, with mention of the Cave of the Patriarchs, caught the attention of the sub-committee, which indicated its opposition to that [arrangement]. The sub-committee also brought up proposals that would allow the police to provide increased enforcement, in the face of disturbances perpetrated by Muslims, to include—on the one hand, giving greater authority to the District Police Commander; and on the other hand, the ability to close the TM/HS to Muslims in light of disturbances coming from their side. The sub-committee did propose methods to increase the number of Jewish visitors, by establishing additional check-points and providing the possibility of visiting the TM/HS on Shabbat. It also shows that political pressure was exerted on the police to allow increased entry of Jews to the TM/HS.

It appears the police are in the middle, between the understanding that placating the Jewish circles to ascend the TM/HS more frequently will lead to more disturbances carried out by Muslims, and will require police allocation of both significant forces and budget, on the one hand, and the political pressure (both overt and covert) exerted on the police to make Jewish ascension possible, on the other.

At the height of the clashes on the TM/HS, MK Miri Regev convened an additional meeting of the committee she headed, attended by then Minister of Public Security, Yitzhak Aharonovich. She opened the meeting quoting the judgment given by the Judge Malka Aviv of the Magistrate Court in Jerusalem on October 4, 2012 in a hearing regarding the extension of the incarceration of Hagai Weiss, who was suspected of attempting to pray on the TM/HS and detained for investigation by police officers who accompanied the group with whom he toured the Mount: "There is room to allow Jews to pray on the Temple Mount," Judge Aviv wrote, adding that, for her, Jews should be permitted to pray on the Temple Mount in a structured manner, in a space designated for that purpose, while maintaining their safety. This, incidentally, was the judge who ruled that the state would pay compensation to Yehuda Glick for preventing his entry to the TM/HS due to suspicion that he would pray at the site.[153]

At that same meeting of the Interior Committee, Aharonovich described the process of the escalation of incidents after the murder of the three Jewish boys who were abducted in Gush Etzion on June 12, 2014, and Operation 'Shuvu Achim' (Come back brothers), that was announced in order to locate them. In addition, there was the murder of an Arab teen, Muhammad Abu Khdeir, and Operation 'Tzuk Eitan' (Operation Protective Edge in Gaza) that followed, along with the Jewish high holidays, which always raise the tension due to increased ascension of Jews to the TM/HS.[154] Aharonovich stated at that same meeting, that in the year 2014, 14 partial closures of the TM/HS, 22 full closures, and 41 restrictions of access were implemented—i.e., closure of the TM/HS to a large portion of Muslims, based on the age criterion being 50 or 55. He added that out of approximately 10,000 Jewish visitors, 1,150 were soldiers.[155]

The assault on Yehuda Glick, Chair of the Temple Mount Heritage Foundation, took place two days after this meeting of the Interior Committee. Glick was shot at and injured severely, after which the police closed the TM/HS to visitation and prayer for a precedent-setting 24 hours, which raised tensions among Muslims.

The desire to improve the status of Jews vis-à-vis the TM/HS, extends beyond fanatic right-wing groups. On June 2014, MK Hilik (Yechiel) Bar, Labor Party Secretary-General, located on the left-center of the political map, was one of the members who submitted a bill strengthening the right of Jewish worship on the TM/HS.[156] Bar claimed that "there is no moral justification for preventing Jews from praying at their holiest site," but three days later he withdrew his support for the bill, following pressure from the leadership of his party. The bill never came to a vote, but Zahava Galon, head of the Meretz party, said that as part of the final agreement it would be right to allow Jews to enter the TM/HS to pray.[157]

The Muslim claim that the increase in Jewish visitation to the TM/HS was a state-sponsored political act, and not just a matter of fanatical groups, stems from the fact that police provide fanatical groups with protection and assistance (this is how the Muslims see it, though in reality the police usually make the situation more difficult for these groups). The Muslim claim also results from the actions of the ministers, Knesset members and Israeli officials who publicly ascended the TM/HS. These actions were documented and published, with reports of the visits reviewed extensively by Palestinians and distributed throughout the Muslim World.[158] Moreover, one Jordanian interviewee by the International Crisis Group claimed that on at least two occasions during 2013-2014, Israel sought permission from the Kingdom of Jordan to conduct Jewish worship in a small section of the site. Jordan, however, refused this request.[159]

Nevertheless, it should be emphasized that despite the rhetoric of elected Jewish officials, and against the rulings of the Israeli courts who ruled that Jews have the right to worship as part of the right of access to the site their holiest site, Israel indeed upholds the principle based on which Jews do not pray on the TM/HS, a principle which the police have enforced throughout the years. The Israeli government makes a distinction between recognizing the abstract and fundamental right of every Jew to commune with his or her maker on the Temple Mount, on the one hand, and bringing about the realization of this right, on the other. For the purpose of maintaining peace, security and public order, Israel has reconciled with the fact that the right of Jews to pray on the Temple Mount will not be exercised.

How was this perceived from the Muslim point-of-view in October 2015? One example shows the Muslim outlook: a moderate businessman from Sur Baher in East Jerusalem said in an interview:

> All the Palestinians believe that Israel wants, one day, to divide the mosques as a prelude to construction of the Temple. This claim has become the true belief among Palestinians for several reasons: The provocative ascensions to the Al-Aqsa Mosque, and the increasing number of those who ascend from amongst the ranks of the settlers, soldiers in uniforms and elected officials, who occasionally pray. Also the subject of archaeological excavations, which Israel refuses to open to international inspection in order to prove it is not carrying out excavations under the mosques, raises deep suspicions among the Palestinians.

The interviewee added to this list: the entry of armed police forces and violent confrontations in the plaza of the mosques, which is considered an integral part of the mosque; preventing Muslim worshippers from entering the site; and a failure to address (and stop) the organizations promoting the construction of the Temple.[160]

The Palestinians claim that the new police directives prohibit Muslims under the age of 50 from entering the Mosque while Jews are on the TM/HS effectively creates separate entry times to the TM/HS between Muslims and Jews "and divides Al-Aqsa Mosque."[161]

Muslims interpret this new situation as official Israeli policy, and not just the actions of small fanatical groups, with the goal of replicating the prevailing situation at the Tomb of the Patriarchs in Hebron. Jordan's King Abdullah II expressed this concern in his statement following the tensions over the TM/HS in the summer of 2015: "Al-Aqsa is the entire Al-Haram al-Sharif, and we accept neither partnership, nor partition."[162] A more radical opinion was that Jews want to take over the entire TM/HS. This spirit was expressed, for example, in the words of Supreme Islamic Authority Chairman, Sheikh Ikrima Sabri: "Entrance of Jews is permitted as visitors, but not as worshippers. Jews call the place the Temple Mount and they say: 'It is ours.' We certainly will not allow them to enter one of our holy sites, to pray there and say that it is theirs."[163]

A significant deterioration in the rights of Jews occurred when the Waqf unilaterally imposed restrictive conditions. Being pressed between the hammer of Israel, who does not prevent the number of Jewish fanatics visiting the Temple Mount, and the anvil of the Muslim Arabs, who see the change on the Jewish side as a danger that could lead to division of the site, the Waqf has worked in recent years to shorten visitation times for non-Muslims by one full hour. Visitors are already guided out of the compound at 10am instead of 11am. Moreover, during the last five years, the Northern Islamic Movement has organized study groups of men and women, whose task it is 'to guard Al-Aqsa from the Jews.' Hamas has transferred funds to the projects of the Islamic movement in Jerusalem, earmarked for religious studies at the TM/HS (Masatib al-'Ilm), aimed at preventing Jews from ascending the Mount. Hundreds of men and women who learned at this site received monthly stipends from Hamas and Northern Islamic Movement sources for performing this task.[164] Their role was to harass Jewish groups during the morning visitation hours while shouting 'Allahu Akbar' [God is (the) greatest]. In 2013, security officials began constricting the actions of these groups, first by closing their sources of funding, and afterward—at the beginning of 2014—by enforcing police prevention of the entrance of the 'Murbitat' (the female group of Al-Aqsa 'defenders') to Al-Haram al-Sharif during morning hours open for visitors and tourists to enter (formally until 11am). Their demonstrations were moved to HaGai Street, close to entrances of the TM/HS. These women's complaints, that they are not being permitted to pray in the Mosque, led to a change in strategy. The police attempted to employ profiling to distinguish between provocative women and other women, and to the latter, provided personalized cards allowing entrance into Al-Haram al-Sharif.

In a discussion of the Knesset Interior Committee, then Deputy Police Commissioner Benzi Sau said, "They singled out 54 Jewish Israelis in Judea and Samaria who endanger public safety and they have been exiled to a variety of communities nationwide. We replicated this same model with respect to 52 youths (Muslims) who were identified as inciters regarding the Temple Mount."[165] In November 2014, Prime Minister Benjamin Netanyahu called for outlawing these groups. Minister of Internal Security, Gilad Erdan, adopted this approach in September 2015, and upon his request, Defense Minister Moshe Ya'alon declared the 'Murabitun' and 'Murabitat' groups 'illegal associations.'

Since that declaration, police have been able to deny entrance to the TM/HS to the harshest activists of the group. Later on, the Northern Islamic Movement was outlawed.

The police also insisted on using all of the time set for visiting hours on the TM/HS. An Israeli police source said that the Waqf attempted to reduce the visitation period to the morning hours alone. However, the police insisted on opening the TM/HS for visitation twice daily, including for an hour following afternoon prayers.

Entrance of Muslims

With the construction of the security fence by Israel in the years 2004-2005, in many cases, worshippers from the West Bank were denied entry Israel, and hence, to Al-Haram al-Sharif. In addition, police were accustomed to restricting entry of young Muslims from East Jerusalem and Israeli Arabs during tense times, during which they received information about the possibility of a disturbance to the public order. In the years 2013-2014, there was a dramatic rise in the number of Fridays during which an age restriction for access was enforced, and the age threshold for Muslims permitted to enter Al-Haram al-Sharif increased gradually, from 40 to 45, to 50 and in certain instances, even went as high as age 55.[166]

As mentioned above, a precedent was set on October 30, 2014: Following the attempted murder of Temple Mount activist, Yehuda Glick, police denied Muslims entry to the TM/HS for 24 hours. In response, Arab East Jerusalem leaders declared a general strike, and Jordan recalled its ambassador from Israel, threatening to sever diplomatic ties with Israel. In the beginning of November, following intervention by U.S. Secretary of State John Kerry, the King of Jordan and the Israeli Prime Minister met. During the meeting Benjamin Netanyahu promised to reduce the tension and allow the entrance of Muslims of all ages from Israel and Jerusalem into the TM/HS compound. In addition, Israel restricted the entrance of religious Jews to small groups (based on their external appearance or in some cases, based on familiarity), and almost completely prevented the entry of government ministers and members of Knesset to the Mount. In reciprocity, the Jordanian Waqf invested efforts to prevent young Palestinians from infiltrating the compound to sleep there at night. Following these changes, violence at the site decreased dramatically.[167] Supervision over Islamic activists was tightened in the holy compound and the surrounding plaza. Israel intensified its intelligence surveillance and added plain-clothed undercover police officers, equipped with cameras to track Jewish groups known to have a history of visiting. This calm lasted approximately ten months, but then the situation reverted back in September 2015, when the police stormed the TM/HS three times, reaching the inside hall of the Al-Aqsa Mosque.

In the year 2012, PA Chair Mahmoud Abbas called on the Muslim World to visit Jerusalem and Al-Aqsa, and thus strengthen the Muslim presence there. Abbas' call reignited the debate among arbiters of Muslim law regarding whether a visit to Al-Aqsa is permitted, under conditions which Israel controls Jerusalem. Jordan encouraged VIP visits of the site. The Chief Mufti of Egypt came to visit Al-Aqsa Mosque, as well as a well-known Yemenite preacher and senior Jordanian officials.

Dress Code and Behavior

Entrance into mosques required strict adherence to proper attire to permit visitation. The Waqf required of female visitors to wear long skirts. The police, for its part, took care that no Jewish ritual objects were brought in, including books.

Security, Policing and Maintaining Public Order

Maintaining security and public order at the TM/HS compound is a complex task. The compound contains nine gates, three of which are open for the Al-Fajr dawn prayer and another four gates open starting at 7:30am. During Ramadan, two additional gates were opened. Thousands of people visit the compound every day, and hundreds of thousands do so in the month of Ramadan. It is impossible to successfully administer a security check at the entrance time for Friday prayers given the quantity of visitors who arrive within a short time. For this reason, there are no basic security measures at the gates, like a magnetometer, to detect metal. It should be noted that before 2003, one police officer was stationed at the gate without a communication device, and only a basic security check was performed.

As of 2014, following the calls of Hamas and the Islamic movement to Muslims to go there and protect Al-Aqsa Mosque with their bodies, many young people came to the compound and spent the night in order to stone the Jewish visitors who would arrive the next morning.

In the years 2003-2005, the Islamic movement intensified its activities on the TM/HS, using offices provided to the movement by the Waqf, within the TM/HS, adjacent to the Mercy Gate. The movement organized festivals with the 'Al-Aqsa Fund' with donations collected from schools.

Local police station at the Northern Wall
(Photo: Author, 2 February 2016)

The adjacent building, Gate of Mercy
(Photo: Author, 2 February 2016)

In 2005, a dramatic change took place in the area of security, maintenance, and policing of the TM/HS. Based on the assessment of security officials asserting that right-wing extremist elements might damage Al-Aqsa Mosque and the Dome of the Rock in order to stop the disengagement from the Gaza Strip and the evacuation of the settlers, Israel invested in upgrading security at the site.[168] At this opportunity, the Northern Islamic Movement offices, near the Mercy Gate were closed by the Jerusalem District Police Commander based on an order to prevent terror. The order was given for six-month periods, and extended periodically.[169]

The police station of the TM/HS, which had been renovated after being burned down in 2000, included a lobby, a commander's office, a conference room and an additional room. The gates and walls of the TM/HS were outfitted with a network of cameras, and the walls were reinforced with a network and remote-sensing technologies. Likewise, the police's forces were reinforced considerably. At sensitive times, the police could call upon not just the dozens of police stationed in the area, but also a special intervention force—and if necessary, a battalion of Border Police stationed at the site, as well as the riot squad. The Jordanians also took measures to strengthen their position in Al-Haram al-Sharif, appointing Azzam al-Khatib, fully loyal to Jordan, to serve in the position of CEO of the Waqf and its board of endowments, replacing the engineer Abd al-Azim Salhab. Jordan added 70 Waqf guardians to the 140 workers already employed in the compound under the command of a retired Jordanian general in 2014.[170] In addition, for the first time, guardians of the Waqf received uniforms (in black).

In 2014, there was a substantial increase in the number of violent incidents and disturbances taking place on the part of young

Arabs who stayed up in the TM/HS at nights. The abundance of violence required police to bolster the unit for the protection of the TM/HS. During that time, Israeli police patrolled the compound more than in the past, especially during visitation hours for non-Muslims. Police escorted Jewish groups visiting the Mount to ensure they did not violate the rules of the status-quo, would not instigate any provocations, and would not be harassed by women's groups (Murabitat) and men's groups (Murabiton)—and recently, children calling out toward them 'Allahu Akbar'. In 2015, police built a transparent fiberglass shield on wheels as protection against stone-throwers barricaded inside Al-Aqsa Mosque.

Mobile defense shield from stone throwing at the Al-Aqsa Mosque
(Photo: Author's collection)

In order to weaken groups of Muslim women and men harassing Jewish visitors on the TM/HS, Israeli police acted decisively and closed some of the entrance gates to the compound early in the hours of the Jewish visitation period. The practical significance of the police decision was a reduction in Muslim access to the compound.[171]

Two issues have yet to be resolved at the time of this writing. Cameras have not yet been installed within the compound—as agreed upon by Israel and Jordan and brokered by U.S. Secretary of State in Fall 2015. Installation of the cameras was prevented at first because of a dispute regarding jurisdiction: who would install the cameras and who would control inspection of the images? When it appeared that an agreement had been reached on installation of the cameras, Jordan rescinded its intention to install them following threats from Palestinian groups that they would target anyone who installs the cameras and would break them.

The second unresolved issue is the installation of telescopic poles with a transparent net that can be stretched between the Temple Mount and the Western Wall Plaza in order to prevent throwing stones at worshippers at the Western Wall. The installation of such a screen is liable to avoid human injuries, and probably, also police intrusions onto the Temple Mount. It is the Waqf who rejects the installation of the net.

Safeguarding the Antiquities and Construction Project

During this period, after 2003, the Waqf continued to not request permits to perform work projects, but rather notified the police of its intentions in an informal manner. The police wrote the requests to perform the work themselves and submitted them to the State's Attorney General and to the Ministerial Committee on Jerusalem Affairs.

In 2007, the Waqf dug a trench on the high stage of the TM/HS for the purpose of laying an electrical cable, and an additional trench, 222 meters across the length of the compound, to replace the electrical cable to the Al-Aqsa Mosque. The work was done with mechanical equipment, at a depth that endangered potential antiquities.[172] This was a violation of the law, although the Waqf coordinated the date of the work's commencement with the Israeli police. The level of supervision of Israel's Antiquity Authority has improved in recent years. A Foreign Ministry official involved in the management of the TM/HS said to the International Crisis Group:

> Cooperation in the preservation of antiquities is now very good. Israel carefully monitors the subterranean spaces. Amman sends requests to us that pass through different institutions within the Israeli bureaucracy. They complain that sometimes requests get stuck at one stage or another for too much time. And indeed, there are those in Israel who delay and postpone providing responses. However, all in all, it works.[173]

Beside the Mercy Gate stands a structure whose top floor serves as Waqf offices for issues concerning the pilgrimage to Mecca (Umra and the Hajj). Its lower portion, which was used by the Northern Islamic Movement, was closed in 2005, as stated in the order of the Jerusalem Police District

Commander. The Waqf requested to renovate the leaking roof and to put in its place the Institute for Studies of the Doctrine of Imam Abu-Hamid al-Ghazali (Muslim theologian of the 11-12 centuries), headed by Prof. Mustafa Abu Sway (who also lectures at Al-Quds University), member of the Jerusalem Waqf and of the Hashemite Fund for Renovation of the Al-Aqsa Mosque and the Dome of the Rock. Israel rejected the request, for fear the Institute would be used to disseminate propaganda and fuel incitement. Therefore, the structure remains empty. This building can be used for offices by a different part of the Waqf, but this is subject to negotiations between the Waqf and the Israeli authorities.[174] It should be noted that outside the building in question lie 3,000 year old wooden beams that were recently discovered. Some believe these beams are remnants of the Cedars of Lebanon used to build Solomon's Temple (and they are lying there untouched, without the benefit of professional conservation).

In the eastern sections of the TM/HS Plaza, between the Western Wall and the Dome of the Rock, among the trees, construction material and sewage are currently situated, which damage the appearance of the space. The Department of Engineering and Construction of the Waqf has a number of metal containers that they use, flanked by large piles of building materials. Beside them, there are piles of umbrellas utilized for shade during the Ramadan. There are also lead cylinders placed in the pile that had been used in renovations of the ceiling in the Al-Aqsa Mosque. These also blemish the appearance of the place.

Lead cylinders from the Al-Aqsa ceiling (Photo: Author, 2 February 2016)

Maintenance Containers, East of the Dome of the Rock (Photo: Author, 2 February 2016)

Water-pressure room, connected to the fire extinguishing faucets, near the maintenance containers (Photo: Author, 2 February 2016)

On the other side lies the debris that was dug out at the time of the opening of the entrance to Solomon's Stables and turned to coal (estimated at 50-100 truckloads). This debris served the Muslim rioters when they came to throw stones at the security forces and Jewish visitors. The Waqf and the police were interested in removing this debris from the Temple Mount; however, in 2004, the Committee for the Prevention of the Destruction of Antiquities filed a petition to the Supreme Court to prevent the removal of the debris and to have it filtered at the site. The State informed the Court that the decision of the diplomatic authority was not to remove the piles of debris from the Temple compound. Therefore, it was agreed upon that if intentions to remove the above-mentioned piles arose in the future, a representative of Israel's Antiquity Authority would notify a representative of the petitioners within a reasonable period of time—and if at all possible, 30 days prior to implementation of the work. In the meantime, the debris has been left untouched, creating both an eye sore as well as a security hazard.[175]

Debris from antiquities at the eastern portion of the TM/HS (Photo: Author, 2 February 2016)

One of the outcomes of the dialogue between the Waqf and the police was the installation of fire hydrants throughout all parts of the TM/HS, including a pump to increase pressure, which was located east of the stage at the Dome of the Rock. Likewise, a fire-extinguishing depot, with a small fire-extinguishing vehicle, was donated by Jordan's King Abdullah II.

Fire-extinguishing depot, west of the Dome of the Rock (Photo: Author, 2/2/16)

In 2012, Israel gave approval for the Waqf to build a structure in the northeastern sector of the stage at the Dome of the Rock, to store the three generators that supply electricity to the compound in the event of a power outage. This was the only building permit given for the TM/HS since 1967. The request was submitted by the police and was approved by the Jerusalem municipality's engineer. Since the structure was made of metal and had no roof, the Waqf now requested approval to add a roof onto the structure (and so far was refused).

The generator farm, to the north of the stage at the Dome of the Rock (Photo: Author, 2 February 2016)

The Palestinians complain that Israel also violates the law. As an example of this, they brought up the inclusion of a fallen stone from the Western Wall in an archeological display at the Knesset. The Palestinian newspaper *Al-Ayam* wrote (on April 7, 2009) that Israel "stole" a stone weighing 5 tons from Al-Aqsa Mosque.

Symbolic expressions and demonstrations
During the period after 2003, the Islamic political movements continued to utilize mass meetings at the conclusion of Friday prayers at Al-Aqsa Mosque as a focal point for protests, raising flags, for the development of slogans and political call-outs and waving banners with nationalistic and political messages.

In summary, since the reopening of the TM/HS to Jewish visitors in August 2003, there have been further violations of the status-quo that prevailed at the site from 1967 until 1996. On the Jewish side, a national–religious organization began to encourage frequent visits in the TM/HS, which was supported by various rabbis and organizations for whom the Temple Mount constitutes a top priority. This activity penetrated the heart of the governmental and public establishments. Some Knesset members began regularly visiting the TM/HS and even encouraged others to do so. The police increased its presence within the TM/HS and helped to exercise the right of Jews to access the TM/HS, without realizing that these increasing visits contribute to changing the status-quo. The Muslims responded to that by organizing shifts to ensure their continued presence at the site and by harassing the Jewish visitors. Thus, the site became the focus of Palestinian political demonstrations, especially at the end of the prayers on Friday afternoons.

Some believe the violation of the status-quo worked mainly for the benefit of the Muslims, which is true. However, those who believe this ignore the increased visibility of Jewish ideological groups visiting the TM/HS compound.[176] The table below presents, for the first time, the status-quo principles of 1967 and the changes that occurred on the initiative of each of the parties.

The Status-Quo of 1967-1996 and its Violation by Both Parties

Field	The Status-Quo of 1967 and onward	Changes implemented by the Muslim Party	Changes implemented by the Israeli Party
Jewish Visitation	4.5 hour visitation window on Sunday to Thursday, through Mughrabi Gate held by police; Ideological visitors enter only in pairs or groups of three.	Unilateral closing in September 2000, and from September 1996 until August 2003.	Forced opening of the site for visitation in August 2003; Entry of more ideological visitors in large groups of 30-50, and visits of political figures.
Visitation Area	Entrance fee for the mosques (only).	Starting from 2003, for Jewish ideological groups only with limited-access (not including the mosques).	
Jewish Prayer	Prohibited	Starting in 2013, harassment of ideological visitors by Al-Murabitun; decreasing closing time by one hour.	Cunning individual attempts of worship and demonstrations of sovereignty through broadcast of internet clips.
Muslim Entry	No limitations and no censorship of sermons	Increase in the number of arrivals since the First Intifada; intensification of incitement in sermons.	Age restrictions; since 2005, prohibition of entry from the West Bank.

Field	The Status-Quo of 1967 and onward	Changes implemented by the Muslim Party	Changes implemented by the Israeli Party
Public Works	With coordination and unofficial supervision	Unsupervised works; police are informed without giving details about work being implemented	Prevention of work, e.g., renovation of building adjacent to Mercy Gate and conditions set by Israel
Excavations for archaeology or for tourism	With unofficial coordination	Dumping of archaeological findings from excavations; creating "Solomon's Stables" entrance and other works harming the archaeology	Opening the Western Wall Tunnel exit; destruction of "Mughrabi Ramp"; digging "Siloam tunnel"; digging "Wilson's Arch"
Site Management	Monopoly of the Waqf	Unofficial involvement of the Islamic movement and external entities	Greater police involvement in decision-making about site closure and other issues
Security and Policing	Israeli monopoly; Waqf employs guards at entrances except for the Mughrabi Gate and inside compound; Israel holds the Al Mahkama building for security purposes	Addition of dozens of Waqf guards through Jordanian initiative	A significant increase in number of police patrolling the compound during Jewish visitation; Policemen breaking into Temple Mount, including Al-Aqsa Mosque, pursuing rioters
Flags	No flags	Used in many political demonstrations, while waving flags and holding banners	
Dress and behavior Codes	According to the determination of Waqf; removal of shoes by visitors at the entrance to mosques and modest attire required for women	Stricter rules in order to make it more difficult for visitors	

CHAPTER 8
Al-Aqsa Crisis and Its Management: October 2015

During September–October 2015, a severe crisis erupted in East Jerusalem against the background of Muslim fears that the steps taken by Israel on the TM/HS were aimed to divide the compound. The Al-Quds Intifada (Jerusalem uprising) was a spontaneous expression of Palestinians who were driven by what was happening in Al-Aqsa Mosque. The events exacted a price in blood and damaged local and regional stability. The violence took the form of another (third) Intifada that included the West Bank and Gaza Strip and endangered the relations of Israel with its strategic partner from east—the Hashemite Kingdom of Jordan.

In response to Palestinian charges, Prime Minister Benjamin Netanyahu said that Israel strictly maintains the status-quo and that the claims against Israel regarding the Temple Mount are nothing but incitement. If there is any party that violates the status-quo, according to Netanyahu, it is the others, by the fact that organized elements of Hamas and the Islamic Movement finance groups that harass Jewish visitors at the TM/HS site. Netanyahu considered the new situation dictated by Israel with its reopening of the site for visits in August 2003 (unilaterally and without Jordan's consent), as a reflection of the status-quo, whereby visitors' entrances to the TM/HS were not coordinated with the Waqf. Palestinian Authority President Mahmoud Abbas demanded restoration of the status-quo of 2000, and that the first step Israel should take to calm the situation should be to stop the visitation of 'settlers' (this is how Palestinians portray the Jewish religious and ideological groups who visit the TM/HS) to the site.[177] It seems Abbas was referring to the situation that prevailed after the visit of Ariel Sharon to the site in September 2000, when visitors were not allowed to enter the site at all, or to the situation that existed before September 2000, whereby the entry of ideological visitors was made sparingly and in coordination with the Waqf. King Abdullah II also demanded the same and claimed that he judges Israel by its actions, not by statements made by its leaders.

The French government initiated a proposal to the United Nations, suggesting that international observers be deployed on the TM/HS, as they were deployed in Hebron, to oversee the implementation of the status-quo at the site. Israel objected to this measure and acted to thwart the initiative together with the United States.[178] Israel also objected to the placement of international entities at the site. To prove that Israel does not seek to divide the Temple Mount for the sake of Jewish prayer (under U.S. pressure), Netanyahu gave formal support of the comprehensive prohibition of Jewish prayer in the TM/HS, in contradiction to the rulings of the courts in Israel, and requested of Knesset members—including Arab members—to refrain from visiting the TM/HS "in the near future." Netanyahu announced he would also prevent ministers from visiting the site during that period. Israel agreed to take some additional steps suggested by the Americans, and on Friday, October 30th, 2015 the age restrictions on the Muslim entry into Al-Haram al-Sharif were removed. Even earlier, police allowed the Murabitat access to the TM/HS again.

On October 24, following meetings with King Abdullah and Chairman of Palestinian Authority Mahmoud Abbas, U.S. Secretary of State John Kerry announced that Prime Minister Benjamin Netanyahu agreed to the Jordanian suggestion to establish continuous around-the-clock surveillance (24/7) of security cameras inside the TM/HS compound. Kerry said Netanyahu pledged to enforce the conduct of the status-quo, according to which only Muslims may pray on the Temple Mount and non-Muslims may only visit. Kerry also announced that Waqf representatives and Israel would meet to discuss calming the situation; that the United States welcomes the increased coordination between Israel and the Jordanian Waqf; and that technical teams of the parties would meet soon to ensure the public order and peace at the site.[179]

The results of the October 2015 agreements, like those of November 2014, indicate again that Israel's ability to exercise sovereignty in the Temple Mount is very limited, and that its unilateral steps resulted in a regression of the situation and to a deterioration of its standing regarding the Temple Mount, compared to the conditions that prevailed before the crisis.

Prime Minister Netanyahu tried to portray the significance of the understandings mentioned above as if the arrangements did not change the order of visitation and management of the site. In addition, Netanyahu asserted that Israel's consent to install the cameras is an Israeli interest aimed at proving who are the real provocateurs at the holy site.[180]

The crisis was managed by the U.S. Secretary of State, who reached general understandings between the three local players: King Abdullah, Abbas and Netanyahu. The statement that conveyed that Jews are visitors and not worshipers at the TM/HS revealed nothing new from a practical point of view, but it was precedent-setting, as an Israeli policy declaration stating that Israel has no intention to bring about Jewish prayer on the Temple Mount. The statement diffused the Muslim concerns that Israel intended to divide Al-Haram al-Sharif. The important part of the statement was the expected coordination between the technical teams of the Jordanian Waqf and Israel to organize the various agreed upon arrangements. In other words: an agreement to that the activities in the TM/HS would be coordinated between the parties, as it had been until 1996.

Palestinian concern regarding potential partition of the site was so weighty, until the Palestinian Authority adopted terminology referring to the entire TM/HS compound as Al-Aqsa Mosque (instead of Al-Haram al-Sharif), and the Al-Aqsa Mosque itself was earned the title of Al-Qibli (the prayer direction, see photo).

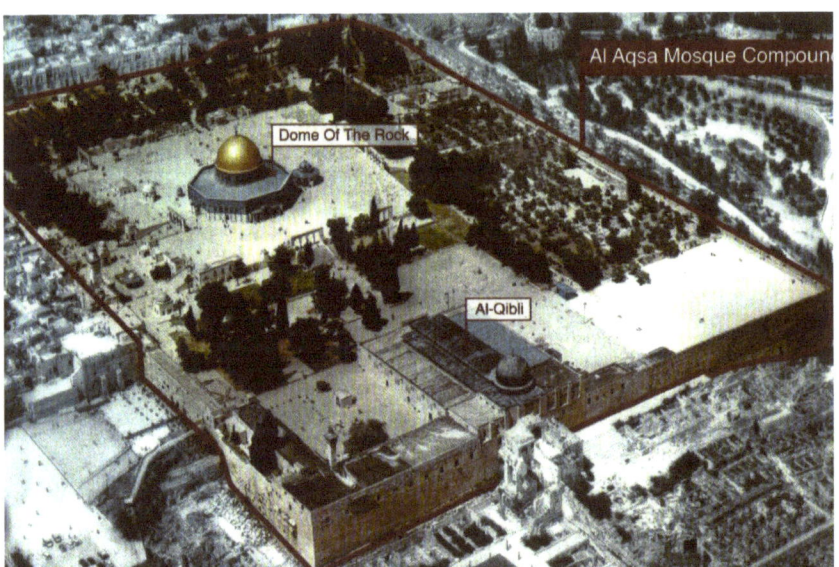

An illustration published by the Palestinian Authority in November 2015. In it you can see the Western Wall, without the Plaza (from the left) (Author's collection)

One week following the above-mentioned understandings, it seemed the police were restricting the actions of Jewish Temple Mount activists, and one of their most prominent activists received a restraining order. The police allowed the Murabitat women to return to Al-Aqsa, but limited their activity to the area of the mosque alone. The number of visitors' groups was reduced to 9 from the 15 it had been before, and according to a *Haaretz* report, 25 Jews who arrived at the Temple Mount on November 1, 2015 did not successfully enter.[181]

At the same time, the understandings of October 24, 2015 are partial, fragile and likely to collapse, as happened when the Waqf requested to place cameras on the site, and then did so without coordinating their installation with Israel. It seems no agreement was reached regarding this issue, as exhibited by the statement of the Jordanian Minister of Religious Affairs, Dr. Hayel Abdulhafez Dawud, to the Jordanian newspaper *Al-Dustour,* that his ministry will be solely responsible for installing the cameras and that management of the project and supervision over it will be the responsibility of the Waqf alone. In his words, the cameras would work 24 hours a day, and the photos would be broadcasted all over the world via the internet, "similar to what is already being broadcasted by the Saudis from the Ka'ba in Mecca, and from Al-Masjid an-Nabawi in Al-Madina."[182]

What is missing in the understandings of October 24, 2015?
The October agreements were a welcome step in reducing the tension. However, they constituted a most limited step, which did not contain the crisis and left too wide of an opening for more crises surrounding the TM/HS to arise. The decision regarding

a dialogue to take place between the technical teams of Jordan and Israel could establish a permanent mechanism of dialogue to preserve the status-quo.

When laying the groundwork for more stable arrangements between the parties, policymakers will need to address following issues:

- The understandings of October 2015 lacked a statement establishing that the status-quo being referred to is the one created in 1967, which remained in place until it began to erode in September 1996, rather than the post-August 2003 situation.
- Whether the status-quo should be officially documented on paper as a basis by which to examine future breaches. On the one hand, some believe that the ambiguity or fuzziness allows Israel a greater degree of flexibility in its conduct. On the other hand, ambiguity serves as a basis for misunderstandings and crises.
- Whether Israel should take steps to restrict ideological visitors. For example:
    - Prohibiting entry of Jewish visitors who belong to religious-ideological organizations to groups of no more than five at one time;
    - Prohibiting visits of groups of soldiers in uniform;
    - Prohibiting government ministers and politicians to ascend the Temple Mount for the purpose of political demonstration during tense periods, or at any other time.

- Should steps be taken to restrict the Murabitun and Murabitat from hindering the visits of Jews, and to remove young Muslims staying in the compound throughout the night?

- Should the parties take steps against financing an entity whose vision includes violation of the status-quo? In terms of Israel, that refers to entities working to establish the Third Temple in place of the mosques, entities that deny the right of Muslims to the site, or entities that prepare curricula encouraging the renewal of Temple worship. For the Palestinians and Jordan, this would mean prohibition of participation and financial support of any entity that denies the Jewish attachment to the Temple Mount. Both sides need to consider whether to prohibit officials who receive salaries from the State of Israel or the Palestinian Authority from expressing opinions that deny either the attachment to the place or the right of the other side regarding the site, and to prohibit incitement by claiming that Israel is acting deliberately to harm Al-Aqsa.

- Should age restrictions on Muslim entry be allowed, and if so, should it be implemented in coordination with the Waqf and/or when the Waqf fails to control the site and prevent any disruption of order?

- Should the parties allow closing the site at the time of serious riots?

- Should the Israeli police be allowed to continue to storm the complex, and if so, should this permission be limited to cases of emergency and conditional upon prior notification of the Waqf?

- Should the parties implement enhanced security measures, like using magnetometers at all entrances or installing a telescopic net on the Western Wall to prevent the throwing of stones from the TM/HS? Should people be prevented from spending the night in the compound? Should construction materials and waste from antiquities remain heaped in the open area to be used by rioters? Should the Waqf be strengthened and reinforced with guards to help keep order at the compound? Should security cameras be installed in the entire complex parts, with a joint command-room or parallel command-rooms?

- Should landscape and physical improvements of the compound be facilitated, as well as permission given to the Waqf to implement additional maintenance and site improvement projects at the compound, including the removal of construction materials and umbrellas from the open area?

These questions need to be addressed in order to stabilize the understandings that were reached through the mediation of the U.S. Secretary of State, so that the status-quo at the Temple Mount will be preserved over time and the site will cease to be a scene of clashes between Jews and Muslims.

Summary and Conclusions

+ On June 1967, a new era began in the history of the TM/HS: For the first time since the destruction of the Second Temple, the Jews had free access to the site, at set visiting times that were coordinated between Israel and the Waqf administrations. Entrusting the Islamic Waqf administration to manage the TM/HS site allowed the two parties to carry out a set of arrangements that—from an Israeli viewpoint—created a new status-quo.[183] However, the Muslims (the Palestinian and the Jordanian) do not officially recognize the new situation, and their reference point to the status-quo is the situation that existed during the period of Jordanian rule, between 1948 and 1967. Both Israel and the Waqf each refer to a different source of authority regarding the status-quo and consider unilateral actions taken by the other side as 'breaches' regarding issues on which previous understandings exist between them. The term "status-quo" at the TM/HS is not meant to refer to a permanent legal and political status, but rather to a description of the *modus vivendi*—the arrangements tacitly agreed upon between Israel and the Jordanian Waqf after 1967, which contain permanent and stable elements on the one hand, and dynamic elements that change in accordance with circumstances, on the other hand.

+ Since the events of September 1996 (following the unilateral opening of the Western Wall Tunnel exit), coordination between the parties became looser, and Muslims gradually gnawed away at the definition of the status-quo by taking unilateral actions and through violence, primarily regarding public works, and sometimes by closing the Temple Mount for visitors. But in August 2003, Israel became an initiating agent, when it unilaterally opened the Temple Mount for non-Muslim visitation, and in contrast to the past, allowed for visits of religious and ideological groups to the site in growing numbers without coordinating with Muslims. This initiative was developed further, with the strengthening of the fanatical Jewish orientation towards the Temple Mount, and the police recently allowing entry of more visitors from those groups, which is perceived by the Muslims as an attempt to take over control and insult the feelings of Muslims. Both parties believed that the other side is the one who was breaching the status-quo. Israel found it difficult to create balanced deterrence towards the Muslims regarding the Temple Mount, which it later exploited to its advantage.

✦ The Government of Israel claims it has full sovereignty over the Temple Mount, but this pretension is impossible to fully exercise, since the Palestinians always have the option of responding with violence. Palestinians' control of the site, and their ability to stir massive crowds to violent protest and to incite the Muslim World with events perceived as offensive to their religious sentiments or breaching of the status-quo, pose a barrier to Israel's ability to exercise its sovereignty, in practice, even in areas seemingly within its authority. Although Israel has the ability to mobilize armed police forces, its capacity to impose its sovereignty is only partial. Israeli authorities are required to employ discretion in every situation that might lead to a confrontation with the

Palestinians. Israel, which claims sovereign authority, stands in such situations facing the question of whether exercising its sovereignty regarding a disputed issue is worth a risk to public order, which may lead to bloodshed, against the harm that could be caused to its standing in the international arena.

As Avi Biton, former Police Commander on the Temple Mount and Commander of the David district said:

> This place has a huge impact, even in more distant circles—e.g., the country's foreign relations and its security. You cannot say you are only interested in what is happening inside the Mount and demand to solve that. You must also address the other circles. We certainly have here a strange situation, but this is a status-quo that we need to enforce.[184]

However, in the continuation of Biton's words in the same newspaper interview, a contradiction arises:

> We evacuate the police station on the Temple Mount in advance of five different occasions: during the four Fridays of Ramadan and on Laylat al-Qadr. This has been done for many years. The purpose of this measure is to prevent posing the dilemma for police regarding whether or not to storm the Temple Mount, and we take into account that our station there might be set on fire. There is no harm to sovereignty here; We are the sovereign on the Mount. Do you think anyone doubts that? When we want, we close it; and when we want, we can storm it. We are fully in control of what happens

on the Temple Mount, and it is important to say that. It is clear to everyone that the game of sovereignty is not a question of whether we are present in the police station or not.[185]

In other words: the police believe that enforcing the sovereignty on the Temple Mount limits its ability to control the entry and exit to/from it. In addition, the police are ready to sometimes sacrifice the police station in order to refrain from having to infiltrate the Temple Mount, fearing the repercussions of what might happen to public safety and the foreign relations of the state as a result. The most outstanding example of the ongoing inability to enforce Israeli law is the failure of the government to implement freedom of worship for Jews on the Temple Mount, for fear that the realization of this right would lead to bloodshed.[186]

✦ Despite its disadvantages, the non-official dialogue mechanism that developed after 1967 between the government representatives and the Waqf leadership provided an effective tool for monitoring, preserving the status-quo and controlling confrontation until September 1996. Harsh incidents erupted on the TM/HS, only when one side asked to implement a unilateral action that the other side could not reconcile. The *modus vivendi*, or the routine matters that evolved between 1967 and 1996, proved themselves as a new status-quo that both parties could live with, although neither party fully achieved its desired goals. Since the events of the opening of the Western Wall Tunnel exit (September 1996), coordination between the parties lessened and their meetings ceased to be purposeful. The continued meetings were intended to preserve the dialogue mechanism, but at that time, Waqf representatives gradually extended their own unilateral control of the site. The meetings were renewed in the recent years, and were conducted at the ground level between Waqf administrators and police officers. At the political level, exchanges are held between a senior Israeli police officer and a Jordanian senior representative.

- Beginning in September 1996, both parties in turn violated the status-quo. The Palestinians claimed that their measures were an attempt to prevent the steps of the Israeli side. For example, the construction of the Marwani prayer hall in Solomon's Stables was intended, they said, to prevent an initiative by Israel's Chief Rabbi, Mordechai Eliyahu, to build a synagogue at the same location.

- Israeli officials believe that the status-quo is limited, mainly in that Jews have free access, but are not allowed to exercise the right to pray, due to the risk to the public safety posed by the Palestinian masses. Israel does not recognize that a dramatic change in the number of Jews ideological visitors, and everything that goes along with that in the field, in the media and in the international arena, might cause a breach of the tacit understandings that are called the 'status-quo'. The violent Palestinian reaction in 2013-2015 was mainly to protest these elements of the status-quo and the fact that the status-quo at the TM/HS eroded, which lead to instability and volatility as long as the situation remained unchanged. The dramatic change in the status-quo following the 2003 reopening of the TM/HS complex to visitors emanated from Israel's unilateral initiative to begin facilitating visits. Following that, Israel decided to significantly expand the groups of religious-ideological visitors to the site. While encountering interference from Muslims, the police did not hesitate to forcefully infiltrate Al-Haram al-Sharif and Al-Aqsa Mosque; in parallel, police restricted the age of Muslim worshipers allowed at the site.

✦ The number of Temple Mount advocates and supporters of the ascension of Jews to the Mount has been increasing dramatically; and in the future, a significant rise in the volume of Jews requesting to ascend the Mount is expected, even hundreds or thousands per day. If no maximum entry quota is set for each population, along with a maximum size allocated to each group, the situation may deteriorate to pandemonium.

✦ The Hashemite Kingdom of Jordan is a central axis in the management and the conflict-resolution on the TM/HS. Jordan's Peace Treaty with Israel grants it special standing at the site, as did the agreement between Jordan and the Palestinian National Authority in May 2013. Jordan was invited by Israel to execute renovation projects at the site and to strengthen the Waqf's control against the forces of the Islamic Movement and Hamas. Jordan is the moderate entity among Muslim stakeholders in Al-Haram al-Sharif. Being considered a guardian of the holy site on behalf of Muslims, Jordan could lose its legitimacy in the Muslim World if Israel takes unilateral action to exercise its sovereignty on the TM/HS. Israel has common strategic interests with Jordan. Therefore, each measure Israel takes on the TM/HS must take into account the implications for its relations with Jordan.

- Israeli police successfully control the entry of non-Muslim visitors to the site and regulate visitation in accordance with the political situation. However, police have been less successful in controlling the visits of Muslims. Time and again, young Muslim troublemakers succeed in entering the TM/HS and barricading themselves inside Al-Aqsa Mosque. Strengthening the power of the Waqf and police cooperation are the most effective tools to prevent the presence of young people in the compound at night. In the long-run, there will be no escape from changing the system of security checks of Muslims at the entrances of the site (despite their arrival in large numbers, in a short time) by introducing numerous check-points before each gate and utilizing magnetometers to check them. It also seems that a telescopic net should be installed above the Western Wall in order to block the throwing of stones over the Western Wall Plaza. A quick solution must be found to remove rubble, stones from the TM/HS, and the construction materials scattered in the open area and put to use by those who disturb public order.

- For the Palestinians, the area surrounding the TM/HS is considered part of Al-Haram al-Sharif in every matter regarding Israeli excavation of the tunnels, the Mughrabi pathway, etc. This fact requires cautious action regarding development work in the TM/HS and its surrounding area.

- Israel finds it difficult to create a balanced deterrent toward Muslims for two reasons: The Muslim position has many players and there is no one controlling entity who can prevent violence in the TM/HS; Mobilizing police forces in a holy and central place for Muslims is considered by Muslims as 'duplicating the occupation.' Moreover, the international community does not recognize Israel's sovereignty over the sacred compound.

+ In order for both parties to be able to refute malicious rumors that one party spreads about the intentions of the other side, the behavior of each should embody respect for the feelings of the other and the ability to calm potential outbreaks, with steps demonstrating they have no intention of harming the interests of each other.

+ Since the unrest is primarily based on religious interpretation, the leaders can mobilize moderate clergy to promote tolerance, reconciliation and the preservation of the status-quo.

Endnotes

1. The term "Temple Mount/Al-Haram al-Sharif (TM/HS), together or separately," as used throughout this study, refers to the area bounded by the wall of the Old City to the East, the southern wall adjacent to the Archeological Park to the South, the Western Wall to the West, and the section between the Gate of the Tribes and Umariyya School to the North. Muslims refer to the compound as "Al-Haram al-Sharif" or "Al-Aqsa". Jews view it as Har HaBayit: the mount of the Jewish Holy Temple, or Temple of Solomon, which once stood within the boundaries of this compound.

2. See the statement of support issued by Religious-Zionist rabbis to Minister Ariel, http://the--temple.blogspot.co.il/2015/09/blog-post_58.html?spref=bl (Hebrew).

3. Iran called for an emergency meeting of the Organization of Islamic Cooperation (OIC), an association of 57 Muslim States and for a response through actions, *Agence France-Presse*, 15 September 2015; Khaled Mashal, head of Hamas's political wing, spoke by phone with Palestinian Authority President - Mahmoud Abbas (Abu Mazen) - regarding the latest events at the TM/HS, Elior Levy, *YNET*, September 15, 2015; the office of Abbas stated that the President had spoken with leaders throughout the world and had asked the international community to put pressure on Israel to prevent confrontations at Al-Aqsa. Turkey's President Recep Tayyip Erdoğan also addressed Israel harshly regarding events at the Al-Aqsa Mosque, and Egypt's President Abdel Fattah el-Sisi voiced concern about the situation as well.

4. The following remarks, for example, were made by a student named Amin at Ibn Khaldun High School in East Jerusalem, during a meeting with Israeli students from a school in the Jewish neighborhood of Pisgat Ze'ev. When the students were asked what they thought about the terrorist attacks in Jerusalem, Amin said, "It is because

of Al-Aqsa... the settlers... they want to build the [Third] Temple." News, *TV Channel 10*, January 4, 2016.

5   *Ha'aretz* website, September 15, 2015 (Hebrew); Diaa Hadid, "Clashes Damage Al-Aqsa Mosque in Jerusalem, and Jordan Warns Israel," *New York Times*, September 15, 2015.

6   U.S. Department of State, Daily Press Briefing, 14 September 2015, http://www.state.gov/r/pa/prs/dpb/2015/09/246874.htm.

7   Regarding the agreement between Abu Mazen and Abdullah, see Elior Levy and Roy Case, "Jordan and the Palestinians Signed an Agreement to Defend Jerusalem," *YNET*, April 1, 2013 (Hebrew).

8   For a summary of these interests see Nadav Shragai's, *The Status-quo on the Temple Mount* (Jerusalem: The Jerusalem Center for Public Affairs, 2016), p. 26.

9   *Ha'aretz*, October 26, 2015 (Hebrew).

10 "The Volcano in Our Hands," *HaMakor, TV Channel 10*, January 5, 2016 (Hebrew).

11 On sacredness in Judaism and Islam see: Yitzhak Reiter, "Narratives of Jerusalem and its Sacred Compound," *Israel Studies* 18.2 (2013) Special Issue: *Shared Narratives — A Palestinian-Israeli Dialogue* (edited by Paul Scham, Benjamin Pogrund, and As'ad Ghanem), pp. 111–132.

12 On the sanctity of the Temple Mount to Christians, see: Yaakov Ariel's "Fundamentalist Christians and the Temple Mount," in Yitzhak Reiter (ed.), *Sovereignty of God and Man: Sacredness and the Centrality of Politics on the Mount* (Jerusalem: The Jerusalem Institute for Israel Studies, 2001), pp. 143–154 [Hebrew].

13 Mujir al-Din al-Alimi al-Hanbali, *Al-Uns Al-Jalil bi-Ta'rikh Al-Quds wal-Khalil*, (Amman: al-Mutkhtasib, 1973), pp.63–65, 113–117.

14 Ibid, p. 67.

15 Aref al-Aref, *Ta'rikh Al-Quds* (Cairo: Dar Al-Ma'aref, 1951), pp. 16, 294; *al-Mufassal fi T'arikh al-Quds* (Jerusalem: Al-Andulus, 1961), pp. 12–13.

16 See: Yitzhak Reiter, *Jerusalem and its Role in Islamic Solidarity*, (Jerusalem: Jerusalem Institute for Israel Studies, 2005), pp. 31-48.

17 See, for example, Menashe Harel, *Three Religions and their Contribution to Jerusalem* (Sha'arei Tikva: Ariel Center for Policy Research, 2005) [Hebrew].

18 *Al-Isra' wal-Mi'raj.* See, Yitzhak Reiter, *Jerusalem and its Role in Islamic Solidarity*, p. 24.

19 On Umar Ibn Al-Khattab in Jerusalem, see ibid, p. 59.

20 See: Amikam Elad, The Status of Jerusalem during the Umayyad Period, *HaMizrah HeChadash*, 44, pp. 17-68 [Hebrew].

21 On Muslim construction in Jerusalem, See: Nimrod Luz, 'Symbols, Landscape, and Ideology in Mamluk Jerusalem,' in *Eretz-Israel, Archeological, Historical and Geographical Studies*, Teddy Kollek, Volume 28, Jerusalem, The Israel Exploration Society, pp. 248-254; Sylvia Auld and Robert Hillenbrand (eds.), *Ottoman Jerusalem: the Living City, 1517-1917* (London: Al-Tajir World of Islam Trust, 2000); Oleg Grabar and Benjamin Z. Kedar (eds.), *Where Heaven and Earth Meet: Jerusalem's Sacred Esplanade* (Jerusalem: Yad Izhak Ben-Zvi and Texas University Press, 2009).

22 http://www.nrg.co.il/online/1/ART2/646/126.html

23 'Riyad Al-Aqsa' elementary school, directed by Akram al-Ashhab; 'Al-Aqsa' high school for boys; and Al-Sharia high school for girls, led by Uhud Sabri (sister of Sheikh Ikrima Sabri, who serves as Chair of the Supreme Islamic Authority).

24 Marlen Eordegian, "British and Israeli Maintenance of the Status-Quo in the Holy Sites of Christendom," *International Journal of Middle East Studies*, 35:2 (May 2003), pp. 307-328.

25 Former Mayor of Jerusalem Teddy Kollek used to say: "the enormous luck of the state of Israel is that Jewish law prohibits Jews from entering the Temple Mount." Mordechai Gur ("Liberator of the Temple Mount,") responded as Deputy Defense Minister in 1992 saying: "One does not for a moment

consider that Jews would be unable pray on the Temple Mount." Gur held that Dayan went too far with the policy he set after 1967, and that it was necessary to restore Jewish ritual at the Temple Mount. At the time of the Washington Declaration, the treaty between Israel and Jordan that the Knesset approved of in August 1994, then-Prime Minister Yitzhak Rabin pledged himself to seek the advice of the Chief Rabbis and the Minster of Religious Affairs before negotiating the Temple Mount. This was the result of pressure from the part of the National Religious Party, as well as Sephardic Chief Rabbi Eliyahu Bakshi-Doron. Some Jews do ascribe to the relinquishing of sovereignty over the Temple Mount. See, for example, architect Dan Darin's opinion piece, "A Mount Against Peace," *Haaretz*, January 25, 2001, B2.

26 See: Special report by the State Comptroller in 2011, not yet officially published, Governmental Decision #761, dated August 20, 1967. It notes that Moshe Dayan saw in the Temple Mount 'a historic site constituting memory of the past' and not a place of current Jewish worship.

27 Yitzhak Reiter, "The Status-Quo on the Temple Mount/Al-Haram al-Sharif Under Israeli Rule (1967-2000)," in Y. Reiter, (ed.), *Sovereignty of God and Man: Sanctity and Political Centrality on the Temple Mount.* (Jerusalem: Jerusalem Institute for Israeli Research, 2001), pp. 297-332 [Hebrew].

28 Ibid.

29 Reiter, Yitzhak, "Jewish-Muslim modus vivendi at the Temple Mount/Al-Haram al-Sharif since 1967". In Breger, M.J., & Ahimeir, O. (Eds.), *Jerusalem: Essays towards Peacemaking* (Syracuse: Syracuse University Press, 2002), pp. 269-295.

30 It should be noted that over 90 parcels of land units on the Temple Mount are listed in the Israeli land register as property of the Muslim Waqf. See Amira Hass, "The Temple Mount is in our hands, Israel claims. Check in the land registry office, reply the Palestinians," *Haaretz,* Sept. 26, 2000, p. 42.

31 Conversation with an individual who requested to remain anonymous.

32 The Waqf Administration was formerly part of the Ministry of Religious Endowments in Jordan, and after 1994, gradually moved to the Ministry of Religious Endowments of the Palestinian Authority, (despite this fact salaries of the Jerusalem Waqf employees were largely funded by the Jordanian government). An Israeli court recognized the title and position of the 'Director of the Waqf in Jerusalem,' and from here, recognition of this position as director of all public Islamic Endowments in the city is derived – with the Temple Mount among them. In spite of the *de facto* recognition by Israeli Authorities of those who fill Muslim positions on the Temple Mount, they do not enjoy any immunity as a result of holding their positions. See: Yitzhak Reiter, *The Waqf in Jerusalem 1948-1990*, (Jerusalem: Jerusalem Institute for Israel Studies, 1991) [Hebrew], p. 17. Regarding recognition of the Waqf Administration, see the court ruling of the Jerusalem District Court 718/69; Sa'd al-Din Al-Alami, *Watha'iq al-Hay'a al-Islamiyya al-'Ulya 1967-1984*, (Jerusalem, the Supreme Islamic Authority, 1984) [Arabic], p. 60.

33 *Haaretz,* July 10, 1988; Interview with Hasan Tahboub, 1988.

34 *Sefer HaChukim,* Book of Statutes, 5727 (1966/7), 449, p. 75.

35 SCJ 2725/93, Gershon Solomon vs. the Chief Commander of the Jerusalem District.

36 Ibid.

37 SCJ 4776/06, Gershon Solomon vs. the Chief Commander of Jerusalem District.

38 Al-Alami, *Watha'iq*, pp. 261-263; *Jerusalem Post*, January 29, 1979.

39 For the rabbinate's ruling regarding entry to the Temple Mount, see, SCJ 4185/90, The Temple Mount Faithful et al vs. the Attorney General et al, *Piskei Din* (5), (1993), pp. 221-288.

40 Interview conducted in 1989, with then mayor Advisor on East Jerusalem, Amir Cheshin. See also: Shmuel Berkovits, *The Legal Status of the Holy Sites* (Jerusalem: Jerusalem Institute for Israel Research, 1997), pp. 174-175.

41 Nadav Shragai and Nina Pinto, "Security Alert, following Confrontation at the Temple Mount," *Haaretz,* August 10, 1999, the headline, p. A1; Nadav Shragai, "The attempt to prevent a fourth prayer site at the Temple Mount," *Haaretz,* August 11, 1999, p. A4; Amira Hass, "Ha-Waqf: 'Israel transmitted false information, to justify its intervention in work projects at the compound,'" *Haaretz,* August 11, 1999, p. A4; Danny Rubinstein, Quick Action at the Tripartite Gate," *Haaretz,* August 27, 1999, B4.

42 SCJ 259/89, 2410/90, *Piskei Din* 48 (2), pp. 256, 352, near letters A-B. Quoted by: Shmuel Berkovits, *The battle for the Holy Places: The Struggle for Jerusalem and Holy Sites in Israel, Judea, Samaria, and the Gaza Strip*, (Jerusalem: Jerusalem Institute for Israel Studies and Hed Artzi, 2000), p. 269 [Hebrew].

43 See the words of Justice Agranat in SCJ 222/68, Nationalist circles vs. the Police Minister, *Piskei Din* 24 (2), p. 141: "It is needless to note ... that the right of the Jews to pray is their natural right, deeply rooted in long history of the Jewish people. In the Supreme Court case of Cohen vs. the Minister of Police SCJ 99/76, *Piskei Din* 30 (2), p. 505, the court accepted as part of the judgment, the prosecutor's response that every Jew has a fundamental legal right to pray at the Temple Mount, provided it is not a prayer of protest meant to cause disturbance to public order." Justice Menachem Elon (a religious judge) ruled in the SCJ 4185/90, the Temple Mount Faithful et al, vs. the State's Attorney-General et al, *Piskei Din* 47 (5), (1993), p.281-282: "every person has the right to freedom of worship, freedom of access to holy sites and to protection against their desecration, which remains in effect in the area of the Temple Mount as well." He also noted, that despite the non-intervention of the court on the question of the realization of the right to worship, this right in itself will forever remain.

44 Supreme Court case, Nationalist circles vs. the Police Minister et al, SCJ 222/68, *Piskei Din* 24 (2), p. 141, made it possible not to permit Jewish prayer. Berkovits, *The battle for the Holy Places,* p. 266, challenges the legality of instructions to police meant to prevent Jewish worship. SCJ 99/76, Cohen vs. the Police Minister from March 21, 1976, *Piskei Din* 30 (3), p.505, established the right of an individual Jew to worship in non-militant prayers, and yet despite this, police

have not made this possible, because any worship could lead to a breach of public order. See Berkovits, *The battle for the Holy Places*, p. 268-269. Englard believed that without a Rabbinate prohibition on ascending the Temple Mount, he is convinced that the Court would have decided otherwise, because the actions of minority groups are contrary to the opinion of the official rabbinic authority. Izhak Englard, "The Status of the Holy Sites in Jerusalem," *Israel Law Review*, Vol. 27, No. 4, (Autumn 1994), p. 598. See also SCJ 1633/93, JDL vs. the Israel Police, and SCJ 292/83, Temple Mount Faithful Association et al vs. Jerusalem District Police Commander, *Piskei Din* 38 (2), p. 449. The court ordered the police to allow the prayer of the Temple Mount Faithful group outside and near the entrance gates to the site. In SCJ 292/83, Temple Mount Faithful Association et al vs. Jerusalem District Police Commander, *Piskei Din* 38 (2), p. 449. See also: Al-Alami, *Watha'iq*, p. 262; On Muslim claims about attempts by Jewish groups to pray on the Temple Mount, an internal memo see *Taqrir Hawla al-I`tida`at al-Isra'ailiyyah ala al-Masjid Al-Aqsa al-Mubarak, Muzakkira Dakhiliyyah*, June 22, 1987, See also: *Haaretz,* August 11, 1989.

45   In the 1990s, political parties began to undertake this struggle. In the guidelines of the new government, established in June 1996, the National Religious Party requested that "the government of Israel arrange for Jewish prayer on the Temple Mount, within the confines of *halacha*." After some discussion, a more general, weaker formulation of the request was approved: "The members of all religions will be ensured freedom of worship and free access to the places that are sacred to them." Publication of these words and their interpretation provoked the Palestinian Mufti, Sheikh Ikrima Sabri, to respond in a threatening tone to any attempt of the Israeli government to allow Jewish prayer on the Temple Mount.

46   See Berkovits, *The battle for the Holy Places,* p. 102, 269-270.

47   Nadav Shragai, "The Temple Mount and the Status-Quo," *Haaretz*, February 2, 1999, p. B3.

48   Nadav Shragai, "Mount of Contention – Jews and Muslims, Religion and Politics, Since 1967," (Jerusalem: Keter, 1995), p. 63. The legal struggle of Jewish groups to exercise their right of worship on the Temple Mount bore fruit, in part, during the 1970s and 1980s. As

the number of incidents with Muslims increased, the direction of the ruling changed as well. On the issue of the right to worship, see: Uzi Benziman, Jerusalem: *City Without A Wall,* (Jerusalem & Tel Aviv, Schocken, 1973), pp. 136-137; Nadav Shragai, *Mount of Contention,* p. 62; Meron Benvenisti, *In Front of the Closed Wall,* (Jerusalem: Widenfeld and Nicholson, 5733/1973), pp. 237-238; *Haaretz,* August 16, 1967.18, 1967; Shmuel Berkovits, *The legal Status of the Holy Sites in the Land of Israel,* (Doctoral Dissertation, The Hebrew University in Jerusalem, 1975), p. 133-135, 161-162, 178; England, "The Status of the Holy Sites", p. 596. On Individual prayer, see SCJ 67/93, The Kach (Kahana) Movement et al, vs. The Minister for Religious Affairs et al; SCJ 99/76, Cohen vs. The Minister of Police, *Piskei Din* 30, 2, p. 505; SCJ 536/81, Anonymous vs. the Israeli Government et al, *Piskei Din* 4, p. 673.

49 Benziman, *Jerusalem,* p. 141-154. However, some operations were exposed by Israeli security forces and by guardians of the Waqf. For example, the intended actions of members of the Jewish underground who were caught in 1984; of the 'Lifta' gang on January 21, 1984; and Yoel Lerner's plan to blow up the Haram mosques in 1989.

50 Al-Alami, *Watha'iq,* p. 500, 535-540.

51 Ibid. pp. 494-496, 530-531.

52 Berkovits, *The battle for the Holy Places,* p. 169.

53 Danny Rubinstein, The Waqf imitated Israel's Method of Operation, *Haaretz,* January 23, 2001, p. A2.

54 Conversation dated February 2, 2016.

55 In the lawsuit submitted by the "Temple Mount Faithful" in 1990, vs. the State's Attorney General and against law enforcement officials it became clear that the Waqf Authority implemented various work projects over the years, without getting permits. Shragai, *Mount of Contention,* pp. 301, based on documents found in the SCJ 193/86 and in Amos Elon, *Jerusalem: Obsession,* (Jerusalem: Domino, 1991), p. 90. The court had the impression that the authorities would excessively turn a blind-eye to violations of the law, nevertheless,

the ruling of Justice Menachem Elon, in essence, sanctioned failure to enforce the law. The judge wrote that he prefers the approach of the authorities that prioritizes reaching an arrangement about the site that leads to respect for the law amongst all of the nationalities and religions, rather than turning the ancient stones into stones of strife. In this case, a precedent was specified citing that flexible and pragmatic considerations, beyond the letter of the judgment, or beyond the letter of the law, are preferable to a hardline approach that is not flexible. The main reason for not interfering with the decision of the authorities was their commitment to maintain close and full supervision of the activities on the TM/HS. SCJ 4185/90, Temple Mount Faithful et al vs. the State's Attorney General et al, *Piskei Din* 47 (5), (1993), pp. 221-288. In March 1988, the Temple Mount *Faithful* filed their first suit for enforcement of the law, in SCJ 193/86. The Waqf was added as a respondent to the first petition, with the consent of both parties. The Waqf claimed that the Court lacked jurisdiction to hear the petition, as the TM/HS, like all of East Jerusalem, is under Jordanian sovereignty and the Waqf does not recognize Israel's sovereignty. See: Nadav Shragai, "SCJ 193/86, Temple Mount Faithful vs. the State of Israel," *Haaretz*, July 21, 1989.

56 Nazmi Al-Jubeh, "1917 to the Present: Basic Changes, but not Dramatic: Al-Haram al-Sharif in the Aftermath of 1967", in: Grabar & Kedar, *Where Heaven and Earth Meet,* p. 257.

57 Yitzhak Reiter and Jon Seligman, "1917 to the Present: Al-Haram al-Sharif/Temple Mount (Har ha-Bayit) and the Western Wall", in: Grabar & Kedar, *Where Heaven and Earth Meet,* pp. 231-272.

58 For claims that the excavations caused physical damage in Al-Haram al-Sharif, see Ikrima Sabri, "Al-I`tida`at ala al-Awqaf wal-Muqaddasat, 1984-1989," in *Al-Mujtama` al-Filastini: Arba`un Aam ala al-Nakba Wahad wa-Ishrun Aaman ala Ihtilal al-Daffa wal-Qita`* (Taibeh: Merkaz Ihya' al-Turath al-Arabi, 1990), p. 50-82. In 1978, Jordan submitted a report to the Director General of UNESCO, charging the excavations were not scientific, but political, and during them, there were attempts to penetrate Al-Haram al-Sharif in several places, and that they caused the collapse of [religious] Mamluk buildings and other historic structures. See Berkovits, *The battle for the Holy Places,* p. 69.

59 Al-Alami, *Watha'iq*, p. 336-338.

60 *Yediot Ahronot*, Aug. 30, 1981; Sept. 2, 1981; Sept. 3, 1981; Sept. 9, 1981; *Haaretz*, Sept. 9, 1981; Quoted by Berkovits, *The battle for the Holy Places,* p. 87.

61 Shargai, *Mount of Contention*, p. 202.

62 Floor of a building, formerly housing a religious institution – Uthman Ibn Affan Mosque – which collapsed above the Western Wall Tunnel, in December 1991. Berkovits, *The battle for the Holy Places*, p. 99; *Kol Hair,* December 6, 1991; *Haaretz,* December 9, 1991; On supervision over the antiquities, see: Shmuel Berkovits, *How Dreadful is this Place: Holiness, Politics and Justice in Jerusalem and The Holy Sites in Israel,* (Jerusalem: Carta, 2006), p. 386.

63 Al-Alami, *Watha'iq*, p. 297-298, *Al-Quds,* December 29, 1978.

64 Berkovits, *The battle for the Holy Places,* p. 72. Based on *Haaretz,* July 10, 1988; July 4, 1988; February 28, 1988; July 22, 1988.

65 On the issue of raising flags, see: Menachem Klein, *Jerusalem in Negotiations for Peace, Arab Viewpoints/Stances,* (Jerusalem: Jerusalem Institute for Israel Studies, 1995), pp. 43-56.

66 Moshe Dayan, *Avnei Derech, Autobiography* (Jerusalem: Idanim, 1976) pp. 165, 498. On the opinions of Israeli officials concerning a flag at the Temple Mount, see Shragai, *Mount of Contention,* p. 306, 378.

67 According to then Chief Military Prosecutor, Meir Shamgar, it was he, who said to Dayan upon his arrival at the Temple Mount for the first time, that this is not appropriate, and consequently, Dayan immediately ordered the flag be removed. See: Meir Shamgar, *Finished, but not Complete,* Tel Aviv: (Tel Aviv: *Yediot Ahronot,* Sifrei Chemed, 2015), p. 86.

68 Thus, for example, there was a procession of the Temple Mount Faithful, October 1989 to be discussed below.

69 Yitzhak Reiter, Third in Holiness, First in Politics: Al-Haram al-Sharif in Muslim Eyes, in Reiter, *Sovereignty of God and Man,* p. 155-179.

70 *Yediot Ahronot,* February 18, 1987.

71 See, for example, an incident from 1989, Minutes of the Knesset, 21, April 11, 1989, pp. 1880-1883.

72 *Maariv,* November 28, 1988.

73 Shragai, *Mount of Contention,* p. 350.

74 Yusuf Al-Natshe, *Al-Marwani Mosque — Between Aspirations of the Past and Hazards of the Future* (Jerusalem: Director of Tourism and Antiquities — The Waqf, 2012).

75 In 1996, the State's Attorney General argued in the Supreme Court regarding planning and building laws, given that the Temple Mount is sacred to several religions, proper interpretation of the terms 'desecration' and 'hurt feelings' should be ... the very existence of a place of worship of a particular religion in a holy site of the same religion, will not in itself constitute a desecration or damage to that place, or to the feelings of members of another religion toward them." The Supreme Court accepted his claim. SCJ 7128/96, *Piskei Din* 51 (2), p. 509. Quoted by Berkovits, *The battle for the Holy Places,* p. 104.

76 Reiter, *Sovereignty of God and Man,* p. 309.

77 According to one participant, Sheikh Salhab expressed his opposition, but did not follow through with threats of mass riots. Minister Shahal did not receive reports of opposition, therefore, he made the decision to recommend opening. See Berkovits, *The battle for the Holy Places,* p. 75-78.

78 According to Berkowits, *The battle for the Holy Places,* p. 104., Arieh Amit wrote his own letter regarding the written consent for the deal and Shahal pointed out to Amit his tactical mistake in this matter. Moshe Sasson, Shahal's advisor, recommended to Shahal to view the letter solely as lip-service, to satisfy the obligation to protest, and that is what he reported to then Prime Minister Shimon Peres. Peres asked Yossi Beilin to examine the issue again with the Waqf. Following Beilin's inquiry, Peres decided not to open the tunnel, which in addition, was not convenient timing from a political perspective in relations with the Palestinians.

79   In the letter, his position is President of the Supreme Islamic Authority is incorrectly listed.

80   I held a conversation on 10/25/1996 with Moshe Sasson, adviser to then Minister of Public Security, who had participated in the meeting. The meeting was attended by many representatives of the police and of the Muslim establishment, including: Hasan Tahboub (Minister of Waqf on behalf of the Palestinian Authority and head of the Islamic Supreme Council.) Sheikh Abd al-Azim Salhab (Chairman of the Board of Religious Endowments), Engineer Adnan al-Husyni, (Director of the Waqf in Jerusalem), . Azzam al-Khatib, (Assistant director of the Waqf in Jerusalem), and Muhammad Nusseibeh.

81   It appears that the municipality issued a decree, not in-conjunction with government officials. *Haaretz,* November 14, 1996.

82   The Mufti, Sheikh Ikrima Sabri, said in a Friday sermon, (September 6, 1996), at Al-Aqsa Mosque, that the Waqf does not intend to honor the stop-work order issued by the Municipality of Jerusalem: "The Al-Aqsa Mosque is outside the authority of this municipality and Waqf officials are not required to get permission from it in order to renovate the site. (*Haaretz,* September 8, 1996).

83   Opening the tunnel was presented by an Islamic research body in Jordan as a change in the character of the city, from Muslim to Jewish. See: *Isra'il Tastawli Ala Bayt al-Maqdis wifqa Mukhattat Istratiji* (Amman: Markaz Dirasat al-Sharq al-Awsat and Dar Al-Bashir, 1996).

84   Al-Jubeh, "1917 to the Present", p. 281.

85   Israeli officials, as interested parties, disseminated false information as if the deal was tied to the Waqf – i.e. that the breaking open of the tunnel was implemented in exchange for allowing the renovation of the Solomon's Stables. See, for example, Nadav Shragai's article, "Who owns the Temple Mount, *Haaretz*, September 19, 1996, written five days before the breakthrough opening of the tunnel because "the Waqf promised to keep peace this time," with the understanding that the Waqf "was intended to prevent a recurrence of the

riots." Jerusalem Mayor Ehud Olmert, (who was among those pushing for the opening of the tunnel), claimed he was unaware of the Waqf's letter of the opposition, and that Shahal had not presented it before the [new] Prime Minister. Berkovits points out some errors in the government's decision: (a) that the Waqf's letter of objection was not brought to the attention of the government; (b) the Waqf was not the controlling authority in the area after the establishment of the Palestinian Authority, and in his opinion there should have direct contact with the P.A., and with representatives of the Waqf; (c) the timing of the action was not fitting (tension on the political front); (d) Prime Minister Benjamin Netanyahu refraining from binding together an explicit deal with the Palestinians: e.g. Opening the tunnel, in exchange for preparing the Solomon's Stables for Muslim prayer. Netanyahu's motives, in his opinion, were a desire to demonstrate that Israeli sovereignty is not dependent on the goodwill of the Muslims (Berkovits, *The battle for the Holy Places*, p.75-78).

86   *Maariv*, October 11, 1996. One of the Justices of the Supreme Court commented in the reasons for rejecting the petition of the Temple Mount Faithful, was that in enforcing the law in a sensitive place, "we should act, beyond the letter of the law". The High Court ruled that there is a necessity for frequent, and ongoing supervision of the authorities inspecting what is being done on the Temple Mount, to ensure that the law is respected. So wrote Judges Gabriel Bach, Zvi Tal and Mishael Cheshin in their decision to reject the petition of the Temple Mount Faithful Movement to enforce the building laws at Solomon's Stables. Judges Bach and Chesin voiced different opinions about law enforcement. Cheshin quoted Talmudic tractate Bava Metzia: "Jerusalem was only destroyed because Torah law was discussed there. In other words: Every one insisted on their own rights, no one conceded their right, and so Jerusalem was destroyed." Let's add: 'The law will puncture the mountain—Let justice be done lest the world be destroyed'?" (*Haaretz*, October 18, 1996).

87   *Haaretz*, October 11, 1996.

88   http://www.arieheldad.co.il

89 Special Report of the State Comptroller, 2011, p. 50.

90 Ibid, p. 4.

91 Ibid, p. 4.

92 Nadav Shragai and Nina Pinto, "Security alert following a confrontation on the Temple Mount," *Haaretz,* August 10, 1999, Headline, p. A1; Nadav Shragai, "The attempt to prevent creation of a fourth prayer space on the Temple Mount," *Haaretz,* August 11, 1999, p. A4; Danny Rubinstein, "Swift action at the Triangle Gate," *Haaretz,* August 27, 1999, B4.

93 Special Report of the State Comptroller, 2011.

94 BerkovitsBerkovits, *The battle for the Holy Places,* p. 49.

95 Nadav Shragai, Archaeologists: An opportunity was missed at the Temple Mount, *Haaretz,* December 26, 1999, p. A8; Nadav Shragai, Aluf Benn and Moshe Reinfeld, "The original permit of the government to the Waqf generally provided for a small emergency opening and not the breaking of two arches," *Haaretz*, December 8, 1999, p. A3; Nadav Shragai, "Rubinstein contradicted the prosecution's position," *Haaretz,* December 8, 1999, p. A3.

96 Special Report of the State Comptroller,2011, p 75.

97 Ibid, p. 54.

98 Ibid, p. 47.

99 Berkovits, *The battle for the Holy Places,* p. 701.

100 Nadav Shragai, "Writers demand (Ehud) Barak prevent the destruction on the Temple Mount," *Haaretz,* June 29, 2000, p. A3.

101 Special Report of the State Comptroller,2011.

102 Ibid, p. 11.

103 Ibid, p. 16.

104 Nadav Shragai, "The Waqf builds and the remnants are destroyed," *Haaretz*, June 16, 2000, p. A2.

105 Baruch Kra, "Chief Rabbinate Agrees: Palestinian Administration of Temple Mount", *Haaretz*, June 28, 2000, p. A1, A21; B. Kra and N. Shargai, "Criticism in the right-wing on the Chief Rabbinate's Approval of Palestinian Management of the Temple Mount", *Haaretz*, 06.29.2000, p. A3.

106 For the opinion of Rabbi She'ar-Yashuv HaCohen, see his article "A house of prayer for all nations," *Haaretz,* August 30, 2000, p. B2.

107 Nadav Shragai, "The Chief Rabbinate will discuss 'concessions in Jerusalem,'" *Haaretz*, December 25, 2000, p. A2.

108 The Chief Rabbis rejected the request from NRP MKs to admit the entrance of Jews to the Temple Mount, *Haaretz,* May 1, 2001, p. 6A.

109 Yizhar Be'er, *Target—The Temple Mount: A contemporary look at the threats to the Temple Mount by Extremist and Messianic forces,* (Jerusalem: Keshev, 2001) [Hebrew].

110 Motti Inbari, *Jewish Fundamentalism and the Temple Mount* (Albany, NY: State University of New York Press, 2007); see also: Motti Inbari, "Religious Zionism and the Temple Mount Dilemma," *Israel Studies* 12, 2 (2009), pp. 27-49.

111 Israel Ariel, *To the House of God we'll go,* (Jerusalem, 2000), quoted in Sarina Chen, "Visiting the Temple, Mount Taboo or Mitzvah." *Modern Judaism,* Vol. 34, Issue 1 (Feb 2014), pp. 27-41.

112 Yizhar Be'er, *Target—The Temple Mount.* See also his updated essay: Yizhar Be'er, *Dangerous Relationship —The Dynamic strengthening Temple Mount movements in Israel and its implications,* (Jerusalem: Ir Amim and Keshev, 2013) [Hebrew].

113 Nadav Shragai, "A Revolution in Religious-Zionist Viewpoint: Dozens of Rabbis Ascend to the Temple Mount," *Haaretz,* May 14, 2007. Supporting this ruling were Rabbi Nachum Rabinowitz, the Rabbinical Council of Judea and Samaria, a group from *'Rabbanei Hillel,'* as well as a group of ultra-Orthodox rabbis, led by Rabbi Yosef Elbaum. Shragai, *The Status-Quo,* p. 31.

114 Chen, *Visiting the Temple*, p. 27.

115 From the Temple Mount News site, http://the--temple.blogspot.co.il/2014/12/blog-post_76.html

116 http://cafe.themarker.com/view.php?t=1153267

117 Miskar Institute, 18 May, 2014, cited by Tomer Persiko, "Why does everybody suddenly wish to ascend the Temple Mount?", *Haaretz*, November 14, 2014.

118 Tomer Persiko, "Why does everybody suddenly wish to ascend the Temple Mount?", *Haaretz*, November 14, 2014.

119 http://the--temple.blogspot.co.il/2012/04/blog-post_3486.html

120 Amnon Ramon, "Beyond the Wall: The attitude of the State of Israel and the Jewish community in all its diversity (1967–1999)" in Reiter, *Sovereignty of God and Man*, pp. 133–142.

121 See for example, the reports and announcements calling for action in: "Let the Temple Be Built," *Journal of the Movement for Establishing the Temple*, 2008, vol. 257, pp. 2–3, pp. 15–16. Online Available HTTP: <http://lamikdash.blogspot.com/2009/02/257.html> (accessed 9 Nov. 2009).

122 See, e.g., the pamphlet "Sovereignty" and the youth bulletin "Small World" on *Balevavot* (Hebrew: Settling from the Heart) website: Online. Available HTTP: <http://balevavot.ios.st/Front/NewsNet/reports.asp?reportId= 222778> (accessed 20 Oct. 2009). Quoted by Eliav Taub and Aviad Yehiel Hollander, "The Place of Religious Aspirations for Sovereignty over the Temple Mount in Religious-Zionistic Rulings," in Marshall J. Breger, Yitzhak Reiter and Leonard Hammer (eds.), *Religion and Politics: Sacred Space in Palestine and Israel* (London and New York: Rutledge, 2012), pp. 139–167.

123 In the beginning of January, to open the 2001, Prime Minister Ehud Barak rejected the request of the Temple Mount Faithful movement to permit visitors to ascend the TM/HS, on the grounds that the security conditions did not allow it. His reply concealed the fact that the true cause of the closure of the site was due to the Waqf inspectors.

124 Ali Waked and Anat Ro'eh, "*Husayni's funeral: Thousands of Palestinian flags in Jerusalem,*" Ynet, June 1, 2001.

125 Luz, p 54. Luz's essay is dedicated to this phenomenon.

126 Efrat Ben-Ze'ev & Issam Aburaiya. Middle ground politics and the re-Palestinization of places in Israel. *International Journal of Middle East Studies*, 36(4), (2004), p. 650.

127 www.Islam-online.net — Under the Notes archive, regarding the actions of the organized transportation. See also: Luz, p. 15 ff.

128 Broadcast on Army Radio evening news, on February 6, 2007.

129 See: N. Hasson and B. Ravid, The Prime Minister ordered the dismantling of the new wooden bridge to the Temple Mount, in response to pressure from the Jordanian royal family, *Haaretz*, September 3; "Reaching Compromise: Why the Mughrabi Gate is a political issue?", September 9, 2014.

130 Aluf Benn, "Israel to Mitchell: The violence was premeditated," *Haaretz*, February 1.2001, p. A6.

131 The High Court ruled in a judgment, by mutual agreement, that the police commander of the Jerusalem district has authority to restrict Jews from entering the TM/HS, if there is probable danger of a severe disruption of order, though it should utilize this authority only as a last resort. The judgment was given on August 3, 1995. SCJ 4868/95, Temple Mount Faithful vs. Israel Police, *Piskei Din* 47 (5), p. 221. On this issue, see: S. Berkovits, *The battle for the Holy Places*, pp. 102, 269-270.

132 Former deputy head of the GSS (General Security Service), Israel Hasson, testified that the holder of the Jerusalem portfolio in the Palestinian Authority Minister at that time, Faisal Husayni, told him that if Sharon does not enter the mosques — there will be no great turmoil. In contrast, the police superintendent, Niso Shaham, former commander of the David police precinct, testified he had warned Sharon and his supervisors that from the Palestinian point of view, the entire area of the TM/HS has the status of a mosque, "Volcano in our hands," *HaMakor*, Channel 10, January 6, 2016.

133   Report on the visit, see, for example, *Haaretz,* September 9, 2000. Estimates by security officials were that if riots erupted, they would be on a limited scale. Palestinian Security Services Chief Jibril Rajoub, warned in advance that the visit is considered a provocation in the Muslim world (*Globes,* September 27-28, 2000). However, according to Public Security Minister Shlomo Ben-Ami, Rajoub said, in retrospect, he estimated that if Sharon refrained from entering into the mosques, no serious disturbances should be anticipated.

134   Scenes of violent incidents in P.A. territories, which caused dozens of deaths and many hundreds of wounded — especially the sight of a helpless child taking shelter with his father from gunfire in northern Gaza, but who was eventually killed, caused his heart an emotional whirlwind. Demonstrations supporting the Palestinians took place in the Muslim world and promoted the sanctity of Al-Haram al-Sharif. (Daniel Sobelman, "Arab countries condemn the 'Massacre at Al-Aqsa,'" *Haaretz,* October 2, 2000.) The riots in the Arab-Israeli sector, which took on the character of civil disobedience, including blocking major highways, burning public facilities and Israeli businesses in the villages, and injuring Jewish bystanders on the roads, and the response of police and security forces, who did not hesitate to use live ammunition to disperse riots, boosted Al-Aqsa Intifadah inside the Green line. Among Israeli Arabs there had been 13 deaths and scores of injuries (and raised the issue of the status of the Arab minority in Israel and the future of relations between Jews and Arabs in Israel to top the agenda).

135   Nadav Shargai, "Negotiations on the mount set a new starting point," *Haaretz,* October 8, 2000, p. A6.

136   Two Palestinians were killed and 24 policemen were injured in the events of October 6th. See Baruch Kra, 'The decision not to bring in police officers to the Mount — contrary to the opinion of Yitzhaki", *Haaretz,* October 8, 2000, p. A6.

137   See, for example, a blogger who writes: "We have lost the sovereignty since we declared during the Six-Day War: "The Temple Mount is in our hands". https://m.facebook.com/story.php?story_fbid=3757931825682626&id=333451253469122&refsrc/ http%3A%2F%2Fwww.google.co.il%2F&_rd (last accessed, December 4, 2015).

138 Daily *TV Channel One* news broadcast, December 22, 2000.

139 Aluf Benn and Amira Hass, "Israeli Source: 'We'll convene direct negotiations'; Palestinians Deny," *Haaretz,* December 18, 2000, p. A2.

140 Report of the International Crisis Group, note 39: The Public Security Minister at the time, Tzachi Hanegbi, claimed that Jordan initially expressed interest in reopening the Holy Plaza to non-Muslims, in coordination with Israel. However, ultimately they gave in to opposition from Arafat, Hanegbi acted without Jordanian consent. Speech by Tzachi Hanegbi, then Knesset Deputy Foreign Minister, November 21, 2014.

141 Arnon Segal, "A Police Officer: It's strange that Jews can't pray at the Temple Mount," *Makor Rishon*, October 10, 2014.

142 http://www.knesset.gov.il/protocols/data/html/pnim/2011

143 Yair Altman, "Because of the advertising: Feiglin's ascension to the Mount was banned," *YNET*, February 12, 2012.

144 http://www.haaretz.co.il/news/politics/1.2731407

145 http://the--temple.blogspot.co.il/2015/09/blog-post_68.html

146 *Haaretz,* November 27, 2015.

147 "Volcano in our hands," *Makor Rishon,* January 12, 2016; *TV Channel 10,* January 12, 2016.

148 Ibid.

149 Broadcast on *TV Channel 10,* photo from the Temple Mount News website; http://the--temple.blogspot.co.il/2013/09/blog-post_2508.html

150 http://the--temple.blogspot.co.il/2013/07/blog-post_1760.html

151 Protocol No. 513 meeting of the Knesset House & Environmental Protection Committee, dated June 23, 2014.

152 Ibid.

153 http://www.scribd.com/doc/257318112/%D7%A4%D7%A1% D7% 9316009-03-11-%D7%92%D7%9C%D7%99%D7%A7-%D7%A0-%D7 %9E%D7%93%D7%99%D7%A0%D7%AA-%D7%99%D7% A9% D7%A8% D7%90%D7%9C (The judgment was handed down on February 29, 2015.)

154 Committee meeting held on October 27, 2014, see: http://main.knesset.gov.il/Activity/Committees/InternalAffairs/Pages/CommitteeProtocols.aspx

155 Ibid.

156 "Bill: Equal civil-religious status for Jews and Arabs on the Temple Mount, June 23, 2014.

157 *Kol Yisrael,* Israel Radio, afternoon news, February 25, 2014, quoted in the Report of the International Crisis Group. p. 14.

158 Report of the International Crisis Group. p. 20.

159 Ibid, p. 20, notes 103-104.

160 *YNET,* October 18, 2015.

161 Ibid.

162 The Jordanian news agency, *Petra*, September 20, 2015.

163 Interview conducted by the International Crisis Group, Jerusalem, May 7, 2014 — Note 11 in its report.

164 Yoav Zeitun, The GSS :Hundreds of young people received a 'monthly stipend' from Hamas to prevent Jews from ascending the TM/HS, *YNET,* May 29, 2014.

165 *Haaretz,* October 13, 2015.

166 Report of the International Crisis Group, p. 8, see also: http://www.jewishpress.com/news/travel-news temple-mount-visits-down-in-2015/2016/01/08/

167 Ibid, p. 10.

168 Conversation with Police Commander Avi Biton, January 28, 2016.

169 Ibid.

170 Conversation with one of the security managers of the Waqf, February 2, 2016.

171 Yoni Mizrachi, *Archaeology in the political struggle over the Temple Mount/ Al-Haram al-Sharif,* (Emek Shaveh/Reaching a Compromise), 2015.

172 Report of the State's Comptroller ,2011, p. 72.

173 Report of the International Crisis Group, note 49.

174 Conversation with Police Commander Avi Biton, February 2, 2016.

175 SCJ 8172/04, Wednesday, Committee to Prevent the Destruction of the Antiquities on the Temple Mount et al vs. Prime Minister of Israel et al (Dr. Shmuel Berkowits or Attorney Yisrael Caspi), by the Israel Antiquities Authority. Turkel, February 15, 2005.

176 See for example, Shragai, *The Status-Quo,* p. 9. Shragai maintains that the status-quo has passed from this world, just that no one has officially announced its burial as of yet.

177 Abbas' words communicated to U.S. Secretary of State Kerry, transmitted through his translator, Nabil Abu Rodayna: http://www.timesofisrael.comisrael-must-maintain-temple-mount-status-quo-abbas-tells-kerry/ 24Oct.15

178 Israeli Ambassador to the U.N. Danny Danon remarked at a press conference that took place at U.N. headquarters in New York, that Israel opposes any international involvement in or supervision over the Temple Mount. http://www.haaretz.co.il/news/politics/1.2753651, October 17, 2015, YNET.

179 *Haaretz* and YNET, October 24, 2015. For Kerry's declaration, see: http://www.state.gov/secretary/remarks/2015/10/248703.htm

180 *Haaretz*, October 25, 2015,

181 http://www.haaretz.co.il/news/politics/.premium-1.2766165

182 *Haaretz,* December 28, 2015

183 The arrangement of the status-quo, in its original context regarding Christian holy sites, gave expression to the balance of power that existed in the past (in the 19th century) between those seeking

recognition of the rights (from Christian authorities) and those who gave them (the Ottoman State). On the status-quo, see: L. G. A. Cust, The Status Quo in the Holy Places (London, 1929,) pp, 3-14.

184 Arnon Segal, "Police Officer: It's Strange that Jews Can't Pray on the Temple Mount," *Makor Rishon,* October, 10, 2014.

185 Ibid.

186 Israeli sovereignty over the Temple Mount is reflected in the following actions: expropriation of control of the Mahkama building (Al-Madrasa Al-Tankiziyya) i.e., the building that was confiscated by the IDF Commander of the Central Command, Rehavam Zeevi, and it was entrusted to Israeli Border Police; Holding the keys to the Mughrabi Gate and gate control, thereby enabling access of non-Muslims to the TM/HS; Overall responsibility for security and maintaining public order; Restricting entrance access to the site based on security considerations; Total blocking or restricting access to the TM/HS during calamity prone days; Involvement in deciding the entrance arrangements and hours of entry into the site, coordinating the visits of VIPs to the TM/HS; Enforcement of Israeli law on perpetrators of offenses committed at the site, and use of force in cases which the government deems to be a serious breach of the status-quo, that suppression of which would create a precedent and a substantial change in the existing situation, or end in violent riots. Along with this, a significant portion of the attributes of sovereignty would not be realized by Israel, and these are: Establishing organized prayer for Jews and implementing freedom of worship for them; Full application of the Antiquities Law and the Law for Planning and Construction; Basic expressions of governance, like raising of a flag and other symbols; Palestinians hold mass demonstrations, waving and hanging national flags and banners with political slogans without approval of the Israeli authorities; Policing and supervision over security and public order are done measuredly, and the Palestinian side, maintains internal guard shifts and shifts harassing Jewish visitors. The Muslim Waqf does not recognize Israeli authority over the TM/HS and views itself as the entity authorized to act as sovereign in the territory of the Haram, but does recognize the Israeli government's responsibility to maintain public order in the compound and to prevent damage being done to it, and this is accomplished through the employment of police.

Bibliography

Al-Alami, Sa'd al-Din (1984). *Watha'iq al-Hay'a al-Islamiyya al-'Ulya 1967-1984*. Jerusalem, the Supreme Islamic Authority. [Arabic],

Al-Aref, Aref. (1961). *Al-Mufaṣṣal fī Tārīkh al-Quds*. Jerusalem: Al-Andalus. [Arabic]

Al-Aref, Aref (1951). *Ta'rikh Al-Quds*. Cairo: Dar Al-Ma'aref

Ariel, Yisrael. (2000). *Beit Hashem Nelech*. Jerusalem: The Temple Institute. [Hebrew].

Auld, Sylvia and Hillenbrand, Robert (eds.) (2000). *Ottoman Jerusalem; the Living City, 1517-1917*. London: Al-Tajir World of Islam Trust.

Be'er, Yizhar. (2001). *Targeting the Temple Mount: A current look at threats to the Temple Mount by extremist and messianic groups*. Jerusalem: Keshev. [Hebrew]

Be'er, Yizhar. (2013). *Dangerous liaison: The dynamics of the rise of the Temple Movements and their implications*. Jerusalem: Keshev and Ir Amim. [Hebrew]

Benvenisti, Meron. (1973). *In Front of the Closed Wall*. Jerusalem & Tel Aviv: Schoken. [Hebrew]

Benziman, Uzi. (1973). *Jerusalem: Unwalled city*. Tel-Aviv: Schocken. [Hebrew]

Berkovits, Shmuel. (1997). *The legal status of the Holy Places in Jerusalem*. (Jerusalem Institute for Israel Studies Research Series No. 73). Jerusalem: Jerusalem Institute for Israel Studies. [Hebrew]

Berkovits, Shmuel. (2000). *The battle for the Holy Places: The struggle over Jerusalem and the Holy Sites in Israel, Judea, Samaria and Gaza District*. Jerusalem: Jerusalem Institute for Israel Studies and Hed Artzi. [Hebrew]

Berkovits, Shmuel. (2001). The legal status of the Temple Mount and the Western Wall in the Israeli law. In Y. Reiter (Ed.), *Sovereignty of God and man: Sanctity and political centrality on the Temple Mount* (pp. 297-336). Jerusalem: Jerusalem Institute for Israel Studies. [Hebrew]

Berkovits, Shmuel. (2001). *The Temple Mount and the Western Wall in Israeli law*. Jerusalem: The Jerusalem Institute for Israel Studies.

Berkovits, Shmuel. (2006). *'How dreadful is this place!': Holiness, politics and justice in Jerusalem and the Holy Places in Israel*. Jerusalem: Carta, 2006 [Hebrew].

Ben-Ze'ev, E., & Aburaiya, I. (2004). Middle ground politics and the re-Palestinization of places in Israel. *International Journal of Middle East Studies*, 36(4), 639-55.

Chen, Sarina (2013). Visiting the Temple Mount – Taboo or Mitzvah, *Modern Judaism*, pp. 27-41.

Cust, L. G. A. (1929). *The Status Quo in the Holy Places*. London.

Dayan, Moshe. (1976). *Avnei Derech, Autobiography*. Jerusalem: Idanim. [Hebrew]

Elad, Amikam (2004). The Status of Jerusalem in the Umayyad Period. *HaMizrach HeHadash* 44: pp. 17-68. [Hebrew]

Elon, Amos (1991). *Jerusalem: Obsession*. Jerusalem: Domino. [Hebrew]

Englard, Izhak (1994). The Status of the Holy Places in Jerusalem, *Israel Law Review*, Vol. 27, No. 4, pp. 587-597.

Eordegian, Marlen (2003). British and Israeli Maintenance of the Status quo in the Holy Places of Christendom, *International Journal of Middle East Studies*, 35:2, pp. 307-328.

Harel, Menashe (2005). *Three Religions and their Contribution to Jerusalem*. Sha'arei Tikva: Ariel Center for Policy Research [Hebrew].

Inbari, Motti (2007). 'Religious Zionism and the Temple Mount Dilemma', *Israel Studies* 12: 2, pp. 27-49.

Inbari, Motti (2009). *Jewish Fundamentalism and the Temple Mount*. Albany, NY: State University of New York Press.

International Crisis Group (2015). *Report no. 159 on the Status Quo at the Temple Mount/Al-Haram al-Sharif.* Jerusalem and Brussels, 30 June, 2015.

Israel State Comptroller (2011). Unpublished Special Report on Implementing Antiquities and Planning and Building Laws . [Hebrew]

Isra'il Tastawli Ala Bayt al-Maqdis Wifqa Mukhattat Istratiji (1996). Amman: Markaz Dirasat al-Sharq al-Awsat and Dar Al-Bashir.[Arabic]

Al-Jubeh, Nazmi (2009). 1917 to the Present: Basic Changes, but not Dramatic: Al-Haram Al-Sharif in the Aftermath of 1967, in O. Grabar and B. Z. Kedar (eds.). *Where Heaven and Earth Meet: Jerusalem's Sacred Esplanade.* Jerusalem: Yad Izhak Ben-Zvi and Texas University Press. pp. 274-288.

Luz, Nimrod. (2007). Symbols, landscape and ideology in Mamluk Jerusalem. In Y. Aviram, Y. Ben Arie, D. Bahat, M. Broshi & G. Barkai (Eds.), *Mehkarim BeYediat HaAretz VeAtiqoteiha.* 248-154 [Hebrew].

Mujir al-Din al-Alimi al-Hanbali (1973). *Al-Uns Al-Jalil bi-Ta'rikh Al-Quds wal-Khalil.* Amman: al-Mutkhtasib. [Arabic]

Natsheh, Yusuf (2012). *Al-Marwani Mosque — Between aspirations of the past and hazards of the future.* Jerusalem: Director of Tourism and Antiquities — The Waqf.

Ramon, Amnon. (2001). Beyond the Western Wall: The relation of the state of Israel and the Jewish public to the Temple Mount (1967-1999). In Y. Reiter (Ed.), *Sovereignty of God and man: Sanctity and political centrality on the Temple Mount* (pp. 113-42). Jerusalem: Jerusalem Institute for Israel Studies. [Hebrew]

Reiter, Yitzhak (1991), *The Waqf in Jerusalem 1948-1990,* (Jerusalem: Jerusalem Institute for Israel Studies. [Hebrew]

Reiter, Yitzhak (2001). The Status-Quo on the Temple Mount/Al-Haram al-Sharif Under Israeli Rule (1967-2000), in Y. Reiter, (ed.), *Sovereignty of God and Man: Sanctity and Political Centrality on the Temple Mount.* Jerusalem: Jerusalem Institute for Israeli Research, pp. 297-332 [Hebrew].

Reiter, Yitzhak (2001). Third in Holiness, First in Politics: Al-Haram al-Sharif in Muslim Eyes, in Y. Reiter (Ed.), *Sovereignty of God and man: Sanctity and political centrality on the Temple Mount.* Jerusalem: Jerusalem Institute for Israel Studies, pp. 155-179. [Hebrew]

Reiter, Yitzhak (2002). Jewish-Muslim *modus vivendi* at the Temple Mount/Al-Haram al-Sharif since 1967 . In Breger, M.J., & Ahimeir, O. (Eds.). *Jerusalem: Essays towards Peacemaking.* Syracuse: Syracuse University Press, pp. 295-269.

Reiter, Yitzhak (2005)., *Jerusalem and its Role in Islamic Solidarity.* Jerusalem: Jerusalem Institute for Israel Studies.

Reiter, Yitzhak (2009). Contest and Co-habitation in Shared Holy Places: Samuel's Tomb and the Cave of the Patriarchs, in Marshall J. Breger, Yitzhak Reiter and Leonard Hammer, Holy Places in the Israeli-Palestinian Conflict: Confrontation and Co-existence. London and New York: Routledge, pp. 158-177.

Reiter, Yitzhak (2013). Narratives of Jerusalem and its Sacred Compound, *Israel Studies* 18.2 (2013) Special Issue: *Shared Narratives — A Palestinian-Israeli Dialogue* (edited by Paul Scham, Benjamin Pogrund, and As'ad Ghanem), pp. 111-132.

Reiter, Yitzhak and Seligman, Jon (2009). 1917 to the Present: Al-Haram al-Sharif/Temple Mount (Har ha-Bayit) and the Western Wall, in B.Z. Kedar and Oleg Grabar (eds.), *Where Heaven and Earth Meet: Jerusalem's Sacred Esplanade.* Jerusalem: Yad Izhak Ben-Zvi and Texas University Press, pp. 231-272.

Sabri, Ikrima. (1990). *Al-I`tida'at `ala al-Awqaf wal-Muqaddasat 1948-1987. In Al-Mujtama` al-Filastini : Arba`un Aam ala al-Nakba Wahad wa-Ishrun Aaman ala Ihtilal al-Daffa wal-Qita`.* Taibeh: Merkaz Ihya' al-Turath al-Arabi, p. 50-82. [Arabic]

Shragai, Nadav. (1995). *The Temple Mount conflict.* Jerusalem: Keter. [Hebrew]

Shragai, Nadav (2016). *The Status-quo on the Temple Mount.* Jerusalem: The Jerusalem Center for Public Affairs.

Taub, Eliav and Hollander, Aviad Yehiel (2012). The Place of Religious Aspirations for Sovereignty over the Temple Mount in Religious-Zionistic Rulings, in Marshall J. Breger, Yitzhak Reiter and Leonard Hammer (eds.) , *Religion and Politics: Sacred Space in Palestine and Israel*. London and New York: Routledge, pp. 139-167.

www.ingramcontent.com/pod-product-compliance
Lightning Source LLC
Chambersburg PA
CBHW041429300426
44114CB00002B/16